From Chaos to Clarity

No Turning Back

Mike Signorelli

Copyright © 2021 by **Mike Signorelli**

All rights reserved. No part of this publication may be reproduced, distributed, or transmitted in any form or by any means, without prior written permission.

Unless otherwise noted, Scripture quotations are taken from The ESV® Bible (The Holy Bible, English Standard Version®) copyright © 2001 by Crossway, a publishing ministry of Good News Publishers. ESV® Text Edition: 2011. The ESV® text has been reproduced in cooperation with and by permission of Good News Publishers. Unauthorized reproduction of this publication is prohibited. Used by permission. All rights reserved.
Scripture quotations marked (KJV) are taken from the King James Bible. Accessed on Bible Gateway. www.BibleGateway.com.
Scripture quotations marked (NIV) are taken from the Holy Bible, New International Version. Copyright © 1973, 1978, 1984, 2011 by Biblica, Inc.® Used by permission. All rights reserved worldwide.

Renown Publishing
www.renownpublishing.com

From Chaos to Clarity / Mike Signorelli
ISBN-13: 978-1-952602-69-6

*To my mother, Sandra, for seeing it in me first.
To my wife, Julie, for reminding me
again and again until I believed.*

CONTENTS

Getting Started 3
Curing Chaos 7
Not Impressed 25
Take Your Ticket 39
It's in the Bag 55
Road to Runway 69
The Ten Enemies 81
Crossing the Jordan 101
Shut Up, Shame! 115
Worship Always Wins 131
Point of No Return 149
Notes 151
About the Author 153
About Renown Publishing 155

INTRODUCTION

Getting Started

I sat in the car outside of a pastor's conference with my wife, Julie, and had a conversation about quitting ministry. I was tired of being misunderstood. I was tired of never making ends meet financially. I was tired of feeling like the total sum of all my efforts wasn't adding up to the life I envisioned. Maybe you've felt this, too?

Julie reached over, placed her hand on my shoulder, and said, "Mike, I believe in your vision to launch a life-giving church, and I won't let you quit." We eventually walked into the conference and attended the sessions.

The final session was taught by Juan Vereecken. As his teaching came to a close, he instructed everyone at the conference to close their eyes. He began to explain that before the conference started, someone in the parking lot may have had a conversation with their wife about quitting their God-dream. I immediately knew I was in the middle of a divine appointment. God was sovereignly speaking to me.

Juan said, "If that was you, grab your wife's hand before we pray because it's time to go V1!" Shaking with awe and reverence for the magnitude of this moment, I grabbed my wife's hand under the table and began to cry.

He went on to explain that V1 is the point of no return. He said that as a plane races down the runway, gaining speed, it reaches something called the decision speed. This decision speed is a point of no return. Once you reach it, the plane is going to fly and there's nothing anyone can do to stop it. The wheels can blow out, the engine can catch fire, but the plane will have liftoff every single time.

I love that metaphor of dedication. Of commitment. Of being all-in no matter what.

And that's why I named my church V1.

I want people to be all-in when it comes to their faith. I want them to reach that point of no return, where they realize that going back to their old ways just isn't possible. They're at liftoff and soaring with God as their pilot.

Within months of making the decision to go all in—V1—I had a team of committed people and finances to begin the process of building the God-dream in reality.

I want this so badly for every person who walks into my church, and friend, I want it for you. I want you to reach a point of no return when it comes to Jesus. I want Him to completely change your life, to take you V1.

The very fact that you've picked up this book tells me that you probably want the same. You're tired of the chains that hold you back. You seek victory, but you've been incapable of fully achieving it for yourself. You're ready for happiness–real happiness. And you know that if you give this Jesus guy a chance, maybe you'll get there.

The Road to V1

In this book, we're going to look at the stories of two men who mentor us through the biblical account of their trials and triumphs: Caleb and Joshua.

Both of these men led the people of Israel into the promised land. They did what Israel had failed to do for decades! Perhaps for generations your family has also failed to step into a life of fullness through Christ. Joshua and Caleb can teach us so much about going V1—about hitting that point of no return and never going back.

While we look at some Bible stories, I'm also going to share about my life and my own path to V1. I was a poor kid in Indiana from a broken home, who God somehow pulled from a life of bad habits and bad decision-making into a life of serving Him as a pastor in New York City.

I'm going to share with you the valuable lessons I've learned while studying the Word and following Jesus. And I'm going to see to it that if you want to, you can make the transition from the road you're on to the runway, and then to V1. At the end of each chapter, workbook sections will aid you in making that transition.

It's going to require some work.
It's going to require some change.
But it's going to be worth it.

CHAPTER ONE

Curing Chaos

I'm in the last generation that had a childhood devoid of the internet. As an eight-year-old, I rode my bike unchaperoned through the treacherous landscape of urbanized Northwest Indiana. I played hard and roamed freely. My mother expected me to be home before dark; that was the beginning and end of my outdoor supervision.

This type of childhood goes up against everything we know today. But you know what? It worked.

Now, I'm not romanticizing the pre-internet era, but I share this so you can understand: life wasn't always as complicated as it is today.

And here's another thing most people don't get: you still have a choice between complicated and uncomplicated.

We are bombarded by messages that tell us we are only a few swipes, clicks, and taps away from wealth. Motivational speeches and self-help programs saturate society. We change careers, work longer hours, marry, divorce, relocate, and do whatever we can to find true identity and calling. We are inundated with cleverly edited content that keeps us on a steady stream of highly entertaining non-essential information. We've heard the cliché, "Knowledge is power," but it seems that for many, *knowledge is paralyzing*. We are trapped in the anxiety of being capable of doing many things yet feeling unsure of how to even begin one thing. As the number of voices in our lives has increased, so has the chaos. We are powerless to decide and commit to the singular aim of our existence. This environment does little or nothing to inspire us to go V1 in our walks with Christ. The fickleness so prevalent in our aimless culture infiltrates our hearts and keeps us from pursuing Jesus to the point of no return.

Dissecting the Chaos

As a child, I was fed a steady diet of empowering messages. From the living room of our tin home in the trailer park, I was mesmerized by characters who would declare, "I have the power," and instantly transform with the ability to conquer any evil. I was convinced that all I really had to do was take my vitamins and say my prayers, and the proverbial championship belt of life's accomplishments would be obtained. In my world, the good guy always won. Only as a teen did I come to the realization that we do not know how to stop mass shootings, terrorism, and the evils of the real world. Even our best heroes struggle to conquer evil.

By my twenties, I'd been through the Boy Scouts of America and public education, and I'd attended a Big Ten University. I was set up for success, and by twenty-five, I had fulfilled the American dream. I had done everything "they" told me to do.

And yet, soon after achieving it all, the cultural myth of success unraveled around me. I found myself in an intense emotional and mental breakdown. I had a house, a family, and a job, yet I struggled to know my true purpose.

Secular humanism, which is a philosophy that looks to human reason instead of to God (or to any supernatural source), leads to an assumption that human beings are the solution to our own problems. That same secular humanistic belief drove me to transcend the extreme poverty of my childhood. That belief demanded I render all excuses void. It didn't matter that my father had walked out. It didn't matter that he moved on, created another family, committed manslaughter, and disappeared from my life. It didn't matter that none of my stepdads ever loved me as their own. It didn't matter that I had to drop out of high school at sixteen to provide for my bedridden mother and four siblings. I just knew I was destined for greatness because that was what society was telling me. I was convinced my life was no exception.

The idea that we can save ourselves is inspiring. But as this worldview plays out in reality, its consequences are devastating.

The movie industry, educational systems, and social media have filled our hearts and minds with the secular humanistic ideology that "all things are possible through the power of self," and yet we are still confused and directionless.

Much of the confusion that we experience is because culture has given us the wrong savior.

Personal Jesus

I was raised in a Christian home. I attended storefront Pentecostal church services many times a week for the entirety of my upbringing, but Jesus' primary role in my life was to empower my own humanistic efforts. I hadn't gone V1 at this point in my life.

Faith in self and faith in God intermingled and produced a wild roller-coaster of emotional fervor. You see, when you believe that Jesus' singular role in your life is to fulfill your own desires, and yet you do not discern the origin of those desires, you've already begun a descent into madness. You end up like me, standing amid the manifestation of all your own hard work—the new car, the house, the family, the college degree, and the career—but with your chaos level increasing as you realize none of those things truly fulfills you.

My failure wasn't a lack of effort or accomplishment. It was that I had accomplished the wrong things for the wrong reasons. I had done what "they" had told me to do and ignored *Jesus*.

I know I'm not alone.

I've talked with many people who went to college because they were told to. They purchased a home beyond their means because it fed a sense of self-worth. They devoted their best years to jobs that fed their bank account. And while they were chasing status and achievement, they starved their souls. That's why they came up empty. That's why *I* came up empty.

The nation of Israel went through a "messy middle." It was a time between their slavery to Egypt and before reaching the promised land. Have you ever been in the messy middle? The people traveling through the wilderness under the leadership of Moses were caught complaining about their hunger, their thirst, and a host of other things. Meanwhile, their wandering led to an entire generation missing the big promise while surrounded by smaller miracles.

By the time the Scriptures record the death of Moses and the transition of his predecessor, Joshua, an entirely new generation was rising up. They watched their parents compromise entry into the promised land by striving in their own strength. They watched their parents miss the supernatural because they were too focused on the superficial.

Joshua and his ally Caleb were different. They honored the legacy of Moses and the previous generation. They acknowledged that being in the wilderness, the messy middle, was still better than being in slavery. But they knew that wholeheartedness, reckless abandonment, radical faith, and being all-in on the big vision of the promised land were the only option. Joshua and Caleb would pioneer the path of uncompromised devotion and surrender to God's perfect will. They would endeavor to do what they had never seen any of their friends or family do: rely completely on God.

Diagnosing the Chaos

I spent so much of my life striving for what the cross of Christ had already won.

Here's what I mean by that. God already has it all figured out. He's already won the battle and conquered death. Because of this, He wants us to operate *from* a place of victory.

I wasn't doing that. I was operating *for* a place of victory. I was chasing after something I felt I needed to earn instead of accepting what God had already done.

My identity was already determined by Christ, but I couldn't see that. My identity was a gift to be received, not a reward to be earned.

In diagnosing my chaos, I had to come to terms with the fact that I wasn't working for Jesus—I was attempting to make Him work for me.

All of my businesses and projects were just serving as a compass pointing toward my true calling, but I couldn't see it even though the evidence was all around me.

I thought I knew the gospel.
I thought I knew God.
I thought I was on a mission.

But it was after I stacked all my accomplishments into a pile and gave them an objective look that I realized I was no better off than when I had started.

My problem was that I had tried to give myself an identity instead of finding my identity in God. I thought my musical ability would make me a rock star. I thought my business ventures would make me an entrepreneur. But our jobs and achievements don't give us our identity. Only God does that.

Socrates famously exclaimed, "The unexamined life is not worth living."[1] I'm suggesting that no amount of examination alone will give purpose to your living. You must receive identity through an encounter with the God who created your true identity before you were born.

You must be willing to shed old mentalities.

You must be willing to acknowledge your own will in order to surrender to the will of God.

You must be willing to address your pain in order to obtain your purpose.

You must be willing to lay aside the expectations of others in order to walk in the approval of God. Moses demonstrated his inability to do this, but Joshua proved it was the only way into the promised land. You'll either seek agreement with people or alignment with God. Moses was constantly trying to appease people, but Joshua and Caleb's generation went V1 by being consumed with the desire to please God.

This isn't a call-out; it's a call-up. God wants to take you into the stratosphere, my friend—the place of God's presence, where striving and trying and chaos are killed. It's a call to go V1, to reach the decision speed at which there is no turning back.

The Cure for Chaos

The account of creation in the Scriptures begins by saying, "The earth was without form and void, and darkness was over the face of the deep. And the Spirit of God was hovering over the face of the waters. And God said, 'Let there be light,' and there was light" (Genesis 1:2–3).

I don't know about you, but I have certainly felt "without form and void." There were times in my past when making something of myself felt so insurmountable. Times when the chaos was all-encompassing. You know what I'm talking about.

When this feeling happens, we go with what's easy, don't we? We walk someone else's predetermined path so that we don't have to deal with what's really going on. We mindlessly scroll social media, hoping that someone will say something to cut through the static humdrum of our nothingness.

But here's the truth about "without form and void." The earth was full of possibility, yet it had no power. It was entirely dependent upon its creator to awaken its true potential. *Think about that.*

The Bible says the Spirit of God hovered over the face of the waters. When you think about the reflective properties of water, this is a powerful image. The earth reflected God's Spirit before He did His work.

Then God spoke. His word was the catalyst for forming the earth into what we know today. And here's the best part: the earth was entirely reliant upon God's creative abilities to become something other than the void of nothing that it had been. The earth reflected the image of

God, and then it was shaped, formed, and given purpose by His word.

The same goes for us. You need God to reflect His image to the depths of who you are. Then you need Him to speak every step of your life into manifestation.

What does this look like in real life? It looks like an encounter with God. To have that, all you need to do is call on Him. It really is that simple. Pledge your allegiance to Jesus and believe that He first loved you, died for you, and ensured that all barriers were broken between you and God.

Take that one step toward Him and He will take a thousand toward you.

Who's in Control?

I wasted many years calling Him, "Father God," while still living like I was master of my universe. I put my trust in money. I put my identity in all I could accomplish. I led worship thinking I was a worship leader. I preached thinking I was a preacher. But life got darker and darker for me.

It was when my biological father died of Huntington's disease that my downward spiral went into overdrive. All I could think of was the possibility that I had unknowingly passed the gene to my daughters. I felt so forsaken, so fragile. My secular humanistic worldview quickly was replaced by nihilism. Since life hadn't created my desired outcome, the only belief I could conjure was that religion is dead and life is meaningless.

And don't forget—I was a pastor and preacher! I was a witness. But in that season, all I could manage was a one-sided screaming match with God.

I had lived so long believing that God wanted me to be the best. I had lived so long believing that He was delighted by my stellar performances. Instead, I felt alone.

I became an alcoholic as I tried to numb the pain, and it was after my wife mustered up the courage to leave me that I finally stood in the quiet of my empty house and offered God the only thing needed to release my true destiny as a son: surrender.

I came to the end of my own efforts. I had done my best and discovered that my best wasn't even what God needed from me. As I literally dropped to my knees, I cried out, "God, I've been an atheist. I've been so mad at You for what I thought was cruelty! I thought that my failures were because You didn't love me. I'm crying out to You now because whether I understand Your ways or not, I cannot deny that You are God, and You rule sovereignly. I may die like my earthly father, but I want to spend every last breath living like my Heavenly Father!"

I still cannot fully explain what happened as I screamed out that prayer. Even though I had been raised in church my entire life—even though I had prayed and preached many times before—this time something was different. It felt like I had accessed the power that comes from the true gospel.

For the first time in my life, I wasn't trying to manipulate the things of God to fulfill my own desires. I was surrendered to God, no matter what. My relationship with Him had nothing to do with what He could do for me. It was based on what He had already done—dying on the cross. I didn't have the language to describe it at the time, but this moment was the first time I experienced going V1 with Jesus.

And I believe this is the *first step* for all of us to go V1. We must recognize that we are not enough and call out to God.

I can't say that everything will suddenly be made perfect. When I came to that V1 point in my life, I still had beers in the fridge that called to my alcoholism. I still had a marriage that was in desperate need of help. But I can say that I had never grasped the full measure of God's grace until I became completely aware of how powerless I was to earn it. That was when my heart opened to my true identity as a son. From there, my entire world shifted out of chaos and into the beginning stages of clarity. My striving ended, and an adventure in being a son of God had begun. I have never been the same since.

Today, I know who I am. I'm a beloved son who sometimes preaches. I'm a beloved son who sometimes sings for the congregation. I'm a beloved son who pastors.

This identity is eternal; it's fixed. I am a son whose assignments change, but my identity remains.

Now, life is a wild adventure. God empowers me to do more than I could have ever done on my own. It may sound like a Christian cliché, but I dare you to try it. I dare you to see what true living looks like.

Joshua and Caleb had a deep sense of identity that was formed in the midst of uncertainty. Because they had watched Moses struggle with the confidence to lead, they undoubtably resolved in their hearts to trust God's plan fully. There's a hidden blessing in having a leader who teaches you what "not to do."

Joshua and Caleb didn't just want a better life; they wanted all that God had for them, too. They somehow understood that if the vision was obtainable through their own strength, then it couldn't possibly be from God. The space between their limited ability and the promise was reserved for the miraculous. The did all they could do, knowing only then would God reveal all that He could do.

A Spiritual Encounter

In the mid-2000s, I attended a national conference for public high school teachers. A renowned futurist was tasked with the responsibility of projecting what the greatest need of students would be in the decades to come. As he migrated through his talk, his speculations were interesting, but they fit with what we expected him to say. Everything made sense in the context of our careers until he reached the end conclusion of his work.

His bold prediction was that the greatest need of the future would be spiritual significance. He said that everything—the data, the projections—pointed to this one need.

There were gasps all over the auditorium. It was as if everyone suddenly realized that the total sum of all their training had failed to address this issue. Technology, globalization, and the ability of most people to meet basic needs meant that students would be searching for more than information. They would desire a deeper experience.

I believe that this futurist was correct. I believe we are living in the reality that he predicted. We have it all! We can achieve it all! And yet, so many feel so empty. Now more than ever, we need spiritual significance—we need to go V1—and that is what I am offering to you.

You cannot solve your own problems. You cannot control the chaos in your life. You will not find significance while chasing after the things this world offers you—money, power, fame. You need an encounter with God. You need the identity that only He can give.

God declared to the prophet Jeremiah, "Before I formed you in the womb I knew you, and before you were born I consecrated you; I appointed you a prophet to the nations" (Jeremiah 1:5). God had a purpose for Jeremiah before he was born—and God has a purpose for you, too.

All you have to do is call out to God. The way in which you do this can be unique to you; the only thing that matters is the state of your heart. In the Bible, one woman broke a jar of perfume over Jesus' feet (John 12:1–8). Another pushed through the crowd just to touch the hem of His robe (Matthew 9:18–26). Others set down their fishing nets (their only source of income) and physically followed Him to the next town (Matthew 4:18–22).

As long as your heart is in the right place, the *how* does not matter. Simply acknowledge your inability to ever be enough. Then find your source in Christ alone as you step into your true identity.

Your assignment—your purpose and the end of your striving—will follow.

WORKBOOK

Chapter One Questions

Question: What is your goal or overall pursuit in life? How is this goal influenced by society's message of success and prosperity? Is it in alignment with God's heart for you and your life?

_____

_____

_____

_____

_____

_____

_____

_____

Question: What experiences in your life have put distance between you and God or made you question and doubt Him? What experiences have drawn you closer to Him? What does this reveal about your trust in God?

_____
_____
_____
_____
_____
_____
_____
_____
_____
_____

Action: *All you have to do is call out to God.* The first step to going V1 is recognizing your need for God and calling upon Him. How you do this is up to you, but intentionally set aside some time to call out to God and allow Him to meet you where you're at.

Chapter One Notes

CHAPTER TWO

Not Impressed

On my second date with my now-wife Julie, I remember thinking that I wanted to marry her.

No joke.

I was smitten and ready to go all-in. And I'll never forget when at the end of that very second date, she dropped me off at my place, and as I moved to get out of the car, she said, "Okay, I love you, bye."

Suddenly, I freaked out. Just moments prior, I had been all-in on the relationship. But that feeling changed the moment she uttered those words. Things got weird.

I started wondering if she was what I call a stage-five clinger. You know, the kind of partner who has to be by your side every moment of every day. I wondered if she was desperate. I wondered if dating her was a good idea.

Of course, Julie looked mortified. She repeatedly told me that she couldn't believe what she said and that it had come out as a habit. But in that moment, I realized that my feelings of being "all-in" maybe weren't as real as I had thought, and that's a good thing. Too much commitment too fast is weird.

But here's what's also true: *not enough commitment after a long time is pretty weird, too.*

You might be going to church, living the Christian life, and doing your thing. Maybe you've been in this mode for a year, two years, or ten years, but you've never fully committed.

You're still dating Jesus; you're still dating His church. And you know what? It's time to get married. It's time to fully commit to what God has for you.

The *second step* in going V1 is recognizing God wants you to fully commit—and committing.

On the Brink of Something Great

I often have this very conversation with people who are frustrated because they aren't able to reach what they've been chasing after.

They can see their dreams, they can see the things that they've been desiring for so long, and yet those things are just outside of their reach.

Have you ever felt that way?

Maybe you played college ball, and you got scouted but never recruited.

Maybe you were in a relationship that you thought was going to lead to marriage, but then it took a turn and ended abruptly.

Maybe you worked so hard and finally got into that career you wanted only to find that the dream was drudgery.

Caleb from the Bible was a guy who faced this very thing. He had been through a lot as he wandered with the people of Israel through the wilderness. They were so close to the promised land—a prosperous land that God had promised to them—they could actually see it in the distance. The only thing standing in their way was that they needed to overtake it.

So Israel sent some spies to scope out the land. Every spy they sent came back with a negative report. Every spy said that the land would be impossible to overtake, that they would surely lose, and that God was setting them up to fail.

Every spy said this, except for Caleb.

> But Caleb quieted the people before Moses and said, "Let us go up at once and occupy it, for we are well able to overcome it." Then the men who had gone up with him said, "We are not able to go up against the people, for they are stronger than we are." So they brought to the people of Israel a bad report of the land that they had spied out, saying, "The land, through which we have gone to spy it out, is a land that devours its inhabitants, and all the people that we saw in it are of great height. And there we saw the Nephilim (the sons of Anak, who come from the Nephilim), and we seemed to ourselves like grasshoppers, and so we seemed to them."
> —*Numbers 13:30–33*

I've read this passage too many times to count, but recently I noticed one incredible thing. Caleb said that they had to go *up*. In other words, they had to go V1. They had to commit fully and allow that commitment to *move* them up and then over.

Of course, he was met with some pushback. "They're so much bigger than we are!" "They're stronger than we are!" You see, that's how the rest of the spies had interpreted what they saw. They saw an enemy that seemed much more powerful than they were, and so they assumed they were toast.

They were willing to abort their destiny because of how something *seemed*. They were about to give up everything that God had been leading them toward for decades, all because of an impression they got during their scouting mission.

How often have you done this in your own life?

"There's no way this is going to work out! I'm too inexperienced, weak, young, old, uneducated, underqualified, ugly, poor, doubtful."

And I'm here to tell you, "No!"

I see a mighty man, a mighty woman of God. You've got a purpose in your life. You're not a grasshopper; you're a giant-killer. And you're going all the way to the promised land—but before you go over, you must go up.

Go up in your integrity.

Go up in your honor.

Go up in your discipline.

Go up in your hunger for the Word. Go up in your prayer life.

Go up in your commitment. Go up in your dedication.

Go up, and then you will go over.

Life will begin to change when you go V1 and rise up, because God is looking for those who have Caleb's heart and spirit.

Accept and Connect

When I show up at my local Starbucks, the baristas there know me by name. They know my order. They know that if they need someone to talk to, they can sit at my table during their break. It's a great relationship. I offer them my counsel, and they offer me free Wi-Fi.

It was during a recent Starbucks trip that I noticed something. I went to connect to their Wi-Fi, and their typical log-in screen popped up. It said, "Free Wi-Fi resources." And to access those, I simply needed to "accept" the terms and then click "connect."

Everything you need to complete your projects and plans and get stuff done is at your disposal. Simply accept and connect.

I've never seen a single person hyper-analyze the terms and conditions of the free Starbucks Wi-Fi. Not once. Everyone accepts and connects, and then they're off. They're V1.

If I had hyper-analyzed the conditions before I accepted what God wanted to connect me to in New York City, I would never have gone. I would have seen the rent in Queens and walked away. Six hundred bucks can buy you a whole lot in Indiana, where I'm originally from. In New York, it doesn't even cover the cost of my daughter's bedroom!

Friend, you don't have to know how it's all going to work out. You don't have to know the ins and outs of where God is sending you. All you have to do is accept and connect. Commit to His plan for your life.

If you could figure out how to finance the vision, there would be no need for faith. If you keep waiting for things to make sense before you commit, you'll be waiting for a lifetime. "Accept and connect" is the formula for faith. The concept is easy, but the implementation will cost you all of your doubts.

I fall short on a number of things, but one thing that I've got down is that I accept before I connect. It's gotten to the point where if I told Julie that I was leaving for Japan tomorrow, she'd pack my bags without any questions asked. She knows, and I know, that when it comes to God, we don't get lost in the details. We accept and connect and trust Him for the rest. When you go V1, there's no hesitation. You're in it for the long haul, and you go where God leads. Faith is an invisible staircase in which the next step only appears as you take it. We've learned this through modeling our lives after the radical obedience of Joshua and Caleb.

Are You a Visionary or a Worrier?

If you filter passion through the lens of negativity, it produces worry. But if you filter that same passion through the lens of positivity, it produces vision.

Vision and worry don't get along.

I think about people in a rowboat. You might have nine people all rowing in one direction, but if there's one person who is facing the opposite way and rowing the opposite direction, then the boat is doomed.

That's the clash between vision and worry. And what we fail to realize is that most people fit into the worry category. They all row as hard as they can, worried about this or that. Meanwhile, the lone visionary is rowing the other way, against the waves that will certainly carry the boat over a cliff.

It was like this with Caleb and the Israelites. The other spies were all worried that they couldn't make it into the promised land, but Caleb was rowing in faith because He could see that what God had promised would come to pass.

V1 people are people with vision. They go against the grain. They have a Caleb perspective on life, and get this: God loves Caleb perspectives!

> But my servant Caleb, because he has a different spirit and has followed me fully, I will bring into the land into which he went, and his descendants shall possess it.
> —*Numbers 14:24*

Like so many others, Julie and I had been hurt while in ministry. After repeatedly being let down, misunderstood, abandoned, and emotionally isolated, we simply wanted to quit for good. I remember telling her in the car outside of the pastor's conference that fateful morning that I was tired of struggling financially to do the will of the Lord. I was tired of making nothing and sacrificing everything. I was tired of ministry. I was tired of suffering. We had spent seven years paying down all our debt so that we could live on nothing and give everything to God, and *I was done*.

We walked into the ministry conference—the conference I mentioned in the introduction—and went to our session, where the speaker stood up and said, "There's somebody here today who had a conversation with their wife in the parking lot here about quitting ministry forever. They want to quit, to do whatever they feel like doing. But I'm here to tell you, it's time to go V1."

It was as if God had divinely disrupted my life to say, "Listen up! It's time to commit!"

My wife and I squeezed each other's hands. We were both crying, and in that moment, it was like the airplane was leaving the runway. We had finally hit the right speed. It was decision time, and we were *in*. In the previous chapter, I had gone V1 in my relationship with Christ. In this scenario, I was being led to go V1 in my calling.

Shortly after that, money started coming to our house in manila envelopes, like we were in the mob. At first, we didn't know what to do—it was so unexpected! But God was miraculously manifesting His church. We were merely the conduits, because we had committed.

Time to Commit

Here's what I want you to understand. When Caleb looked at the giants, he wasn't impressed. You see, he had seen the Red Sea part. He had seen God lead His people using a cloud by day and pillar of fire by night (Exodus 13:21). He had been fed by manna that had fallen from the heavens every time he got hungry (Exodus 16). He had seen all of this and more, and so when he spied on the people of Canaan, he wasn't impressed.

Caleb must have been thinking, "*Sure, those guys are tall, but do you remember the size of the waves when God parted the sea? Did you see the height of the pillar of fire that guided us through the dark every single night? Our God is stronger.*"

When I went V1, I had a similar experience. I looked at our finances. I looked at the impossibilities of starting a church in New York City. And I had to say, "*God, You were with me back when this all started, and You're going to see me through.*"

It's time we start to make the words "not impressed" part of our vocabulary when facing opposition on our journey with Christ. Just like Caleb wasn't impressed by what he saw in Canaan, we shouldn't be impressed by what stands between us and God's best.

If you just got diagnosed with cancer, I want you to say, "*I'm not impressed.*" Your Savior literally robbed death and rose again on the third day.

If you're looking at the slip from the bank that says they're repossessing your house, say, "*I'm not impressed.*" They can take your house, but they can't take your salvation, your joy.

It's time we stop being impressed by the devil and what he's trying to do. It's time we stop being impressed by people who don't have God at the top of their call list. It's time that we say, "*I'm not impressed,*" to the giants that stand in the way of the destiny God has for us. God wants that from us. He wants us to rest in Him, to trust Him, to not be shaken, to accept and connect and go V1.

It's time to shift your thinking. It's time to view God as more than something you dabble in on the side. It's time to open yourself up to the possibility that God wants you to be all in, and He has so much planned for you once you can get to that point of full commitment.

It doesn't matter what your friends think. It doesn't matter how ticked off the devil will become. The only thing that matters is that you fully commit to God and His destiny for your life.

WORKBOOK

Chapter Two Questions

Question: The Israelites were willing to abort their destiny because of how something *seemed*. Have there been circumstances that caused you to want to turn back in your walk with God? What were they? How does that affect your relationship with God today?

_____
_____
_____
_____
_____
_____
_____
_____
_____
_____

Question: Have there been times in your life when you wanted to give up your Christian faith, ministry calling, or something else related to your walk with God? Did God show up for you during that time? How did that change your perspective? What does that reveal about God's nature?

_____
_____
_____
_____
_____
_____
_____
_____
_____
_____

Action: *God wants you to fully commit.* Write a letter to God. Confess all your fears and hesitations and worries. In the letter, acknowledge that God is bigger and set your heart to fully commit to Him.

Chapter Two Notes

CHAPTER THREE

Take Your Ticket

I started a bacon festival in Northwest Indiana. We had ten thousand people in attendance before one o'clock the very first day of the very first year we held the festival. Every store within a ten-mile radius of the event was completely sold out of bacon. It was like a movement! People weren't merely showing up for the event. They weren't just attending for a bit and then moving on with their lives. They were committed to bacon!

As we discussed in the previous chapter, commitment is imperative to going V1. And I want you to understand this: *there is a difference between involvement and commitment.*

When it comes to God, involvement isn't enough. *Trying* isn't enough. What He wants from us is commitment that is active. We don't have to be perfect—Jesus used a ton of imperfect people.

The *third step* in going V1 is being fully, actively committed to God every single day. That's what God wants from you.

You see, I'm not the most eloquent person. I'm not the best writer or the best storyteller. I'm not the best preacher the world has seen. I'm probably not even in the top ten thousand.

But the reason God has put me in the place that I'm in is because I've gone V1. That's it. That's the secret sauce.

Take Your Ticket

> But my servant Caleb, because he has a different spirit and has followed me fully, I will bring into the land into which he went, and his descendants shall possess it.
> —*Numbers 14:24*

Let me take you back to the year 2000, when I was a teenager. The time of frosted blond tips, JNKO jeans and downloading Dave Matthews Band on Napster.

My mom had a nighttime dream that she just couldn't shake. In her dream, a big white airplane landed on our street and came to a screeching halt right in front of our house. Then she woke up.

From 2000 to 2003, she had a reccurring dream that she was in an apartment. There were all these boxes, and all five of us kids were storing up our childhood memories in these boxes. All of a sudden, the Holy Spirit spoke in the dream, saying, "Sandra, leave these boxes, leave these childhood memories, leave this apartment, leave this house, go get your ticket, and then get on the plane."

She had this dream for *three years*. It was so strong it became part of our family culture. We *still* can't get together without mentioning the dream.

Well fast-forward seventeen years. I started a church called V1. Of course, you know the significance between that name and airplanes, but it's so much more than that. I started the church in a theater that is across the street from an airport. I didn't know it when I was signing the contract. I simply went for a walk, and there it was. An airport.

I moved my family from Indiana to New York, and I went to my mom and my stepdad, Papa Dean, and I asked them to move with us to help watch our kids while Julie and I started this church. Papa Dean wasn't very interested in New York, but I felt strongly that they should come with us. So I prayed about it.

There are times when you will have a deep conviction and it will align with Scripture. When that happens, it's a powerful thing. Every sign I was getting from God was that my mother and Papa Dean needed to join us in New York. I felt like if he stayed in Northwest Indiana, he was physically going to die.

The next day, I called him, ready to plead my case. He stopped me before I could begin. He said that God had awoken him in the night and told him that he was going to New York. He said God had said that if he *didn't* go, he was going to die in Northwest Indiana.

It took my breath away. It was one of those God moments that is so much bigger than we are.

They started looking for places to live on Long Island, and their realtor was a Jewish woman who had accepted Christ as her Messiah. She was showing my mother and stepfather a potential place for them to live when she asked them to hold on. She then turned to my mom and said, "Sandra, I have to say something to you. I don't think I've ever heard God before, but I think I'm hearing Him right now. God says it's time to take your ticket, Sandra. God says it's time to take your ticket."

In that moment, my mom and Papa Dean knew that they were right where God wanted them. God had been threading this needle for seventeen years. He had started this dream all the way back in the year 2000.

My mom fell to the ground and started crying. She had finally received closure on the dream she'd had seventeen years prior.

This kind of a story is always fun to tell and fascinating to listen to, but I can almost predict the way people will react. Most think that it's a great story, but they doubt that such a thing could ever happen to them.

Let me be very clear: friend, you are in a divine appointment right now. It is by no mistake that you're reading this book. It's by no mistake that you are looking for deeper connection.

God has a plan for your life. It's not about being the most intelligent or the most talented person in the room. It's about being a doer of God's Word, and the ticket price to get into His kingdom is commitment.

But what does commitment look like? It's one thing to make a head-decision to commit. It's another to make a life decision that affects you every day. Let's look at

Caleb again to discover more about this kind of daily V1-level commitment.

Caleb's Commitment

> *Then the people of Judah came to Joshua at Gilgal. And Caleb the son of Jephunneh the Kenizzite said to him, "You know what the LORD said to Moses the man of God in Kadesh-barnea concerning you and me. I was forty years old when Moses the servant of the LORD sent me from Kadesh-barnea to spy out the land, and I brought him word again as it was in my heart. But my brothers who went up with me made the heart of the people melt; yet I wholly followed the LORD my God. And Moses swore on that day, saying, 'Surely the land on which your foot has trodden shall be an inheritance for you and your children forever, because you have wholly followed the LORD my God.' And now, behold, the LORD has kept me alive, just as he said, these forty-five years since the time that the LORD spoke this word to Moses, while Israel walked in the wilderness. And now, behold, I am this day eighty-five years old. I am still as strong today as I was in the day that Moses sent me; my strength now is as my strength was then, for war and for going and coming. So now give me this hill country of which the LORD spoke on that day, for you heard on that day how the Anakim were there, with great fortified cities. It may be that the LORD will be with me, and I shall drive them out just as the LORD said."*
> —*Joshua 14:6–12*

This passage is Caleb's perspective on his life. In it he talks about the things he went through, the things he had seen. And I believe there are seven truths that he teaches about commitment.

1. Commitment increases your capacity. If you say *yes* completely, with all your heart, your capacity will increase. I can tell when someone's not fully committed to something; it's revealed in their actions. If you have a spouse, then you know this is true! You stick with them, even when there are problems, and that's because you're committed. And when you're committed, you're able to shoulder a whole lot more and put up with a whole lot more than when you aren't.

2. Commitment demands attention. We don't shine the spotlight on people who do something great one single time. We shine the spotlight on people who continue to perform over and over again. Great leaders don't become known for their leadership after doing one good thing. They become known for their leadership after they've shown a commitment to it—after they've stayed the course through thick and thin. You see, people may not notice you the first time. They may not listen the first time. You can be telling your friends and family about this Jesus who can radically save their lives, but the key is that you've got to say it again and again and be committed in your life, not just your words. That's when people take notice.

3. Commitment generates credibility. We count on people who are consistent. The mailman will always deliver the mail. Your child's schoolteacher will always show up to teach. Commitment produces credibility.

4. Commitment makes way for God's promises to manifest. He wants to give you everything that He's promised you, and commitment allows Him to do that!

5. *Commitment is a choice that produces a feeling, not a feeling that produces a choice.* You want to know why your dad walked out on you? Because he defined commitment as a feeling. You want to know why people have abandoned you? Why they've left you high and dry? It's because they didn't *feel* like being committed to you anymore. When feelings determine what we do, then we fall short. But when our actions—our commitment—determines how we feel, then we stay true.

I can just imagine Caleb as an eighty-five-year-old man. A bit weathered. A bit hunched over. But ready to kill giants. He was committed to God, and that determined how he felt. His passion didn't waver. He was the same man at eighty-five that he had been at forty. He was ready for whatever God had for him, because he was committed.

6. *Commitment gives you the ability to see what others will never get to see.* I started this journey of ministry with some people who aren't even in the game anymore. They walked out. They quit. And they have missed so much. They have missed seeing the hand of God move in unbelievable ways. They've missed lives being changed, blessing being given, doors being opened. I've seen all of these things and more, because I am committed. If you quit too soon, you miss out.

7. *Commitment reveals the depth of your conviction.* People change their minds all the time. One day we like someone; the next day we're not too sure. One day we're putting all we have into one vision; the next day we've got a new idea that has our full attention. There is some-

thing to be said for someone who sets up camp and stays put. Someone who is willing to fight every single day, without giving ground, without giving up, without being swayed. Someone who believes their calling so much, they're willing to risk it all. Now that's some heavy stuff, and I totally get it!

Commitment might be foreign to you. After reading this list, you may feel as though you've never fully committed to anything in your life, but there's something interesting I want to point out about Joshua 14:6. Caleb was a Kenizzite, which was another way of saying that he wasn't an Israelite.

You see, at some point in time, one of Caleb's ancestors had a revelation that the God of Israel was the true God, and that revelation caused that person to make a decision. Consequently, they switched teams. They moved from being Kenizzites to Israelites. They took their ticket and got on the plane. And generations later, their descendant Caleb—who wasn't supposed to be there to begin with—was calling the shots.

Maybe you don't know a lot about theology, or you don't know much about the Bible. You don't have it all figured out, but you feel God pushing you. You feel Him calling. You see something real about God's church, and you want to grab hold of it even though you feel like an outsider.

Sometimes it takes somebody stupid enough, crazy enough, bold enough to be the outsider who says, "You all see a defeat, but I see a victory because I'm not looking down. I'm looking up."

Friend, if this is you in any way, it's time to go V1.

Everything will change when you commit—your marriage, your finances, your trajectory. And even if you lose it all, it's still a win. In 2 Timothy 2:11, Paul wrote from jail, saying that if he died with Christ, he'd be living with Christ. If you stick it out, you'll rule, my friend. If you stay to the end, you'll win no matter what.

Commitment Issues

When I was twenty-one years old, I was standing in a hotel lobby in Orlando, Florida. I was getting ready to marry my wife, Julie. We were stupid, and we were in love. I'll never forget her coming down in her wedding dress and veil. All of a sudden, we were looking into each other's eyes. I'll never forget the moment she said her vows, "for better or worse, for richer or poorer." When it came to be my turn, I'll be honest, I don't think I knew what I was saying or doing. I didn't understand the depth of the commitment or what it would look like to stay committed on the road ahead.

But Julie knew. And she has walked it out every single day since.

After that day, we went on a long journey in which I had to learn what commitment is all about. You see, if you're wounded and fatherless and have abandonment issues like I do, it's a bit hard to understand commitment. No one had modeled it clearly for me. Nobody had taught me.

Nobody, except for Jesus.

He lived two thousand years ago, and He's here right now through the Holy Spirit. He said, "I will never leave you nor forsake you. I am with you always, to the end of the age" (Hebrews 13:5; Matthew 28:20). He said it then, and He's saying it to you right now. *Jesus* will model commitment for you.

The other day, I listened to Simon Sinek give a talk in which he said there are organizations that are structuring themselves around creating an unfireable culture.

Think about it. Our culture is so abandoned and orphaned that we're creating unfireable work cultures.

People don't want a boss; they don't want a leader or a guru. They want a father, someone who will accept them back no matter what. Who will stay with them and correct them and teach and guide them. Someone who will love them when they have it all together and love them when they don't.

Twenty years ago, when I first started studying leadership, the entire focus was on the word *leader*. Now we're in the era of mentor, mentor, mentor, and what that really boils down to is *father*.

A leader can cast you aside when you're not producing or not at your best. But a father says, *"You are mine. No matter how far you run, I will chase you."*

That's what our world craves, and that is exactly what our Father in heaven offers. But you must take your ticket; you must accept your role as child. You must go V1.

Stay the Course

Let me tell you about a man who found a rock stratum that he thought might contain gold. It had all the indicators; it checked all the boxes. He spent thousands of dollars and years of his life digging for what he believed was there. Finally, he got discouraged. It had been so long, he'd dug so deep, and he'd come up with nothing. So he sold the mine to someone else. That buyer dug for three more feet and hit gold.

Too many times in life, we give up too soon. But Caleb shows us what can happen when you commit daily and keep pushing. God is opening the door to show you your purpose, to show you what He has for you. Will you start walking that purpose out every day?

You will never be what God has called you to be until you commit. He's committed to you, but you need to enter into the relationship, too. You need to actively participate. An airplane that sits still on the runway will never go V1. You have to start moving.

You may have distanced yourself from the church. You may have condemned yourself and stopped using your ministry giftings, stopped serving. You may be isolated and cold to the loved ones around you, but God is telling you right now to commit. You may have struggled with commitment all your life, with your family, your job, and your marriage, but God is telling you to start here. Commit here. The rest will fall into place.

He hasn't abandoned you. He's been waiting all this time with the plane running, ready for liftoff.

Commitment happens every day. It's step by step. You choose to commit today, and then tomorrow you'll have to choose to commit again.

Julie and I renewed our vows once I actually figured out what commitment meant. When we did this, we invited all the haters and everyone who didn't think that we were going to survive in our marriage. Everyone who gossiped about us, everyone who doubted us. We invited them to the ceremony, and we all took communion together.

Communion is a beautiful thing that reminds us of what Jesus did on the cross, and through that communion, there is forgiveness. We asked God and one another for forgiveness. The blood of Christ washed us clean. His broken body healed our wounds. He brought back to life a marriage and relationships that had died.

To commit, all you have to do is ask God to wash you clean. Ask Him to forgive you. Claim His promises on your life and receive what He has to offer you. Then, by faith, believe it.

Do this today, and do this tomorrow. And the day after that.

WORKBOOK

Chapter Three Questions

Question: Do you believe God has a plan for your life? Looking back, in which moments can you see the ways God has consistently been involved in your life and guiding you?

_____
_____
_____
_____
_____
_____
_____
_____
_____
_____
_____

Question: What is the difference between a head-level commitment and a commitment that transforms your life? Is there evidence in your daily life that you are committed to your relationship with God? If not, what needs to change?

_____
_____
_____
_____
_____
_____
_____
_____
_____
_____
_____

Action: *Be fully, actively committed to God every single day.* As you allow God to bring you to the point of V1 in your walk with Christ, make spending daily time with God a priority. Set a specific time every day and intentionally spend that time with God.

Chapter Three Notes

CHAPTER FOUR

It's in the Bag

When I first came to New York, I was looking for every strategy possible to reach people. All I wanted was to love people with the love of God. I had a heart of desperation, wanting people to know the true God, to know that He isn't an old guy with a white flowing beard, peering out from the heavens and judging you.

God is *with* you. Right now.

When Jesus left this earth, He sent the Holy Spirit to stay with us. Through the Holy Spirit, Jesus is unlimited. When He was in a body, He could only be in one place at a time. He could only heal the people who were with Him. He could only reach the people He could see and talk to.

But when He unleashed His Spirit, He was able to be everywhere—and not only that, but He is also able to dwell *inside us*.

So my mission when I came to New York was simple: get the people of Long Island to know that Jesus loves them so much that He wants to have a relationship with them. I wanted to see the people of New York go V1 for Jesus.

Not too long ago, I was on the phone with a Google Analytics expert. He was based out of Texas, where it seems that everyone is a Christian. He pulled up Long Island to look at web stats.

He went neighborhood by neighborhood. Twenty-thousand people here. Thirty-thousand people there. And then he pulled up how many people in the neighborhoods had done a web search related to looking for a church. The results? Two people in one town, a couple people in another. Zero people in another.

I was shocked; he was discouraged. He said that the numbers of people looking for a church in the Long Island area were so low, he couldn't promise me that we would see anything close to the web traffic results we were looking for.

When he said that, my heart sank. I cried out to God, wondering how I was going to accomplish His mission of reaching people and telling them about His love if the people weren't even interested to begin with. This struggle stirred in my spirit for a few days.

I was working back at the church headquarters when the front door began to shake so loudly that I thought it was going to come right off its hinges. A woman on the other side was banging on it, yelling to us that there was an emergency and that we needed to call the cops.

We opened the door, and she told us that her car was on fire. She needed help. Sure enough, about fifteen feet from our building, her car was completely engulfed in flames.

So we got her to safety and called for emergency help. I remember turning to her and asking if she was okay. She said she had left an important briefcase in the car, but that the *most* important thing was that she and her husband were safe. In that moment, the Holy Spirit spoke to me in what would be a game-changing moment in my life.

The Spirit pointed out that our headquarters didn't have a sign, so there was no way she could have known what we were about, what we were trying to do there. The Spirit told me that when people's lives are on fire— when there is an emergency and they don't know where else to go—they're going to come looking for the people who have the answers. And if you have Jesus, you have the only answer that makes sense.

Those web stats presented a huge obstacle. But over the years, that obstacle has become our greatest strength. It's *because* no one in New York is looking for a church that we have been able to make a fresh start. You see, no one has expectations! We don't have to play church or do anything just to please the people walking through the doors. We don't have to play the part of religion. Instead, we offer a relationship with the very One who established the church.

I've found that I'd rather work with a whole bunch of misfits and people who don't know Scripture very well over the ones who fit in, look like church people, and know theology. I love watching as God makes his church out of nothing. Many times, it's the broken, the battered, the incomplete people whom God chooses to use.

It's that very brokenness that positions you to go V1. The *fourth step* to go V1 is to trust God with the broken pieces of your life.

Promise for the Future

> *And Joshua the son of Nun and Caleb the son of Jephunneh, who were among those who had spied out the land, tore their clothes and said to all the congregation of the people of Israel, "The land, which we passed through to spy it out, is an exceedingly good land. If the LORD delights in us, he will bring us into this land and give it to us, a land that flows with milk and honey. Only do not rebel against the LORD. And do not fear the people of the land, for they are bread for us. Their protection is removed from them, and the LORD is with us; do not fear them." Then all the congregation said to stone them with stones. But the glory of the LORD appeared at the tent of meeting to all the people of Israel.*
> **—Numbers 14:6–10**

Let me give you a little bit of context here, because the history of the children of Israel, God's chosen people, is so very important. They had been living in captivity, as slaves, in Egypt. Pharaoh was a cruel taskmaster who had them work all day long and gave very little in return. He beat the ones who didn't comply, and he rooted out rebels.

So God, using Moses, brought them out of that captivity and promised them a new life in a new land. The journey there was arduous, but in this passage, they were actually close enough that they could see the promised land in the distance.

If you've ever used a promise of something great to motivate yourself in the here and now, then you should be able to relate to what was going on there. If you've ever shopped at Goodwill, promising yourself that once your career turns around you'll shop at Nordstrom's, then you know what I'm talking about. If you've ever told your kids to be patient with Mommy's work schedule because one day she'll be a certified nurse and things will be better, then you know what I'm talking about. Promises of a better future help us in the here and now. They help us to do the things we don't like and work jobs that we hate.

So when it came to Israel, it was as if God was saying, "Look, I know slavery was hard, but I promise that one day, I will give you a land that flows with milk and honey." This had been the promise all along. It had been what drove Israel and brought them back to the center every time they went wayward. Now in this passage, they finally got to see what God had been talking about all along. They were close enough to see the promised land.

The Language of Certainty

IKEA seems to be the only furniture store that is in everyone's budget. I swear my whole bedroom set cost me $17.50 and came in fourteen separate boxes. Of course, then I opened the boxes and found out why it was seventeen bucks in the first place. Inside was nothing more than raw wood, a chisel, and a hammer. There should have been a note that said, "Good luck, Mike!"

But I'm a big IKEA fan, so we decided to get all of our furniture and the things we needed for headquarters there. My parents came over to help put things together while I ran around, doing lots of other things related to launching and managing a church. And I'll never forget how at the end of the day, I returned and my mom handed me a bag. It was all the leftover parts.

Now, if you're a leader, you know about something called volunteer tax. There is no such thing as free labor. Even if someone volunteers their time, it's still going to cost you because they'll mess something up or break something or require lots of supervision.

So, when she handed me the bag, I knew I was in for it. Because you and I both know that when it comes to IKEA, there aren't supposed to be any leftover pieces.

Life is like this, too. You do your best and try your hardest, and yet you still feel destroyed. Life is so hard. Then you come to church and realize there are all these pieces left in the bag. Painful things that linger, things that maybe you could have done better. Those items sit in the bags we carry with us when we go to God.

Thankfully, God has given instructions for how to do life. It's all lined out for us in Scripture, but we don't always follow Him, do we? We do things our way, and that's when we leave pieces in the bag.

This bag is a much bigger deal than we give it credit for. If you can't figure out what your purpose is, it's because you have pieces in the bag. Maybe you get stubborn and obstinate, and you want to do it your way. You don't want to read the instructions, because you think the Bible is outdated. You think it doesn't jive with modern science and philosophy. So instead, you watch three YouTube videos and think you know the meaning of life!

But when you come into God's Kingdom, when you become a Christian, you learn the language of the Bible and of God's heart. You stop speaking the language of fear and doubt and worry, and you start speaking the language of certainty.

Caleb spoke this language. He said that God would bring them into the land, no matter what. It was a promise.

We've all been let down by broken promises in the past. Maybe it was a spouse who walked out on you or a boss who didn't give you the raise they had promised. But the promises of God come from certainty, and Caleb knew this. He had seen God work. He had seen God's faithfulness.

Caleb had certainty because he had gone V1, but the rest of Israel? They had left God in the bag. And it took all that Caleb had to remind them that, *"We've got it in the bag!"*

Fear No Evil

> The LORD is my shepherd; I shall not want. He makes me lie down in green pastures. He leads me beside still waters. He restores my soul. He leads me in paths of righteousness for his name's sake. Even though I walk through the valley of the shadow of death, I will fear no evil, for you are with me; your rod and your staff, they comfort me. You prepare a table before me in the presence of my enemies; you anoint my head with oil; my cup overflows. Surely goodness and mercy shall follow me all

> *the days of my life, and I shall dwell in the house of the LORD forever.*
> —*Psalm 23*

Every plane starts on the ground. Before the engines turn on, before it rumbles down the runway, it starts at a low point. You might be able to relate to this. Maybe you're at a low point right now. You're in a valley.

The thing is that we can choose how we talk about our situations. We can say that we're in despair—or we can say that we're on the runway, about to take off.

This is the language of certainty. It's the language of Caleb, saying, *"God will give us this Promised Land!"*

This passage goes on to talk about the valley of the shadow of death. The interesting thing about this is that the *shadow* of death is not actual death. It's the projection of threat.

Many times the things that are chasing us down are just shadows. We ask for God to remove them, because we're so scared, but He is training us. He's teaching us. He's showing us how to stand in the midst of that fear and become who we've been destined to become.

Then the verse says to fear no evil. Now stick with me here. If your soul is a combination of your mind, your will, and your emotions, then as a true Christ follower, you will soon learn that your feelings lie to you.

You see, another definition of "will" is "decision maker." There is evil on the earth because people make bad decisions all the time. They make bad decisions because of free will. But we can also choose to make good decisions. We can choose to fear no evil, and the Psalmist gives tells us why.

For You are with me.

If you're reading this today and God is not with you, you have every reason to be afraid. Matter of fact, you should be terrified. You see, I tried to do life without Christ, and it's not pretty.

But once you invite Him into your life and commit to fearing no evil because He'll be with you, then you'll have His rod and staff helping you. For many shepherds, a rod has come to be associated with correction while a staff is used to guide.[2] These were two distinctly different tools with different purposes. The prodding of the sheep with a rod was a method for dealing with stubbornness. A sheep in forward motion only needed a staff for direction. But a stubborn sheep, perhaps one suffering from the paralysis of analysis, needed the prodding of the shepherd's rod to create breakthrough.

I can't tell you how many men I have sat down to counsel, and have corrected and rebuked and disciplined, telling them the truth even though it was hard. And then these men weep. They have never had anyone in their life care about them enough to be honest with them, to discipline them, to call them out.

A pain worse than discipline is the absence of God—when He leaves you alone and turns you over to your own reprobate mind. Romans 1:28 warns us that "since they did not see fit to acknowledge God, God gave them up to a debased mind to do what ought not to be done." People often ask, "Where do you see the goodness of

God in the story of Job, Pastor Mike?" He lost everything, including his family, health, and possessions!

It's simple: God never left Job alone. Job suffered much, but acknowledged God in all things, and saw restoration. Job received the rod and the staff of correction and guidance, and after his repentance the Bible records that God blessed his latter days more than his beginning (Job 42).

If you're going through a valley, if you feel like you're in the low place, just know you are getting ready for takeoff. Those broken pieces left over from when you tried to assemble your life? Bring them to God. He has a purpose to take you V1. He has put everything you need in the bag.

It's in the Bag

God's promise to Caleb was the promised land.

What promises does He have for your life? What could you accomplish with Him by your side, with His rod and staff there to correct and guide?

You might have convinced yourself that there's nothing worth saving when it comes to your life. You might have convinced yourself that you're too broken or too far gone. Maybe your bag of parts is more like a whole storage unit of missing and broken pieces. Maybe there are voices in your life telling you you're not worth it or that it will be too hard, too painful to change.

Or maybe you have big dreams that you think can't possibly come true. They're too dangerous. They're too difficult.

God has the pieces in the bag. He has the pieces to your life and the pieces to your dreams. Let Him put you back together.

It starts with a prayer. When you realize that God is in control, suddenly the pressure is off. Things don't begin and end with you. You are not the master of your own future! And you don't have to be afraid.

Yes, we have free will. Yes, we can choose good or bad, but we also have a Father in heaven who has the pieces in the bag.

So pray to Him. Admit to Him that you don't have it all figured out. That you want His will, not your own. Tell Him that you surrender. You don't need the right words to say. You don't need to have your life together. There's nothing magic about this prayer, it's the intent that matters. When you mean the words that you say, then everything will change for you. Bring Him the broken pieces of your life and watch Him equip you to go V1 for His glory.

WORKBOOK

Chapter Four Questions

Question: Has God given you any promises that help you stay faithful even when times are challenging? Write those promises as a reminder of God's goodness in your life.

_____
_____
_____
_____
_____
_____
_____
_____
_____
_____
_____

Question: What can you accomplish with God by your side? What are the broken pieces left in your bag? Have you given them to God? Do you know He wants to use you?

_____
_____
_____
_____
_____
_____
_____
_____
_____
_____

Action: *Trust God with the broken pieces of your life.* Write your dreams on a piece of paper. Ask God to show you His dreams for you and write those down, too. Surrender to God's will, believing that He can take your broken pieces and bring His purposes to pass in your life.

Chapter Four Notes

CHAPTER FIVE

Road to Runway

On a recent Black Friday—you know, the day after Thanksgiving in which people go shopping and stores offer great deals—there was a guy who went shopping at Target. He walked in, wearing a red shirt and khakis, and suddenly a store manager told him to get to work. He handed the guy a nametag and had him start scanning things.

The guy was shocked. He couldn't believe what was happening, so he started live-tweeting it. He scanned for hours. He even asked for a break and was denied!

This surprise employee was tweeting at Target, too, asking them what they were going to do about the fact that they'd hired him without knowing whether or not he wanted to work there.

What's funny is they called on him to work, and for whatever reason, he was willing. He wasn't trained or qualified, yet he started scanning items when they told him to scan items!

When you read the Bible, you'll find that the qualification for God to use people to do great things was just one condition: willingness.

Some of the greatest things God has done through me happened before I got trained. This is because God uses the foolish things of the world to confound the wise (1 Corinthians 1:27 KJV).

You may not feel qualified to do what God is asking of you, but are you willing? If the answer is yes, get ready for God to take you from road to runway.

A Heart for the Runway

Right now, you are either on a road or you're on a runway. Roads are long and frustrating. A two-thousand-mile road trip is a two-thousand-mile road trip. You can drive as fast as possible, as recklessly as possible, and you still won't beat a plane once it has left the runway. If you are living your life in your own strength, you will never experience the liftoff that comes on the runway. Living your life on the runway is what happens when you surrender your life to the power of God's Spirit. He will accomplish things in your life that you never thought possible.

Most of us spend our time on the road, but we were meant for the runway. You were meant for the runway.

The *fifth step* in going V1 is saying yes to the runway. Don't keep living on the road going only as far as your strength can take you.

This is a choice you have to make. The most deceitful thing in your life isn't your backstabbing friend or your lying ex or your dysfunctional parents. The most deceitful thing in your life is your heart. The Bible says, "The heart is deceitful above all things, and desperately wicked" (Jeremiah 17:9 KJV).

I have counseled people one-on-one in closed-door settings for almost twelve years. And I will tell you this. To have a clean heart in the twenty-first century is something that's earned, not something given.

The heart has corridors, and if any of us are honest, when we explore the corridors of our heart, we find rooms that we've given to God and rooms that we're keeping for ourselves. There are memories we give to Him and memories that we hide from Him. There are events that we give to him and events that we cover up.

But the Bible is clear that Caleb served wholeheartedly from a place of surrender. And once his plane left the runway, he never looked back. Caleb's heart was put on display when he caused a silence to fall over all the people before Moses and said, "Let us go up at once and occupy it, for we are well able to overcome it" (Numbers 13:30).

Immediately after making this bold declaration that the impossible is possible with God, the same people who spied out the promised land with Caleb revealed they had a different mindset. Their bad report ended up becoming the official narrative to the masses. When you live a life of surrender to the impossible, don't expect it to be the most popular message. You'll find that fear travels faster than faith in most circles. This did not deter Caleb. He was resolute in the certainty that God meets us at our level of expectation. Therefore, when Israel did eventually step onto the soil of the promised land, Caleb's wholeheartedness was established as the only way into the God-dream.

God took Caleb and used him, an outsider, to transform His people and lead them to the promised land. Here's the singular reason why in Numbers 14:24, "But my servant Caleb, because he has a different spirit and has followed me fully, I will bring into the land into which he went, and his descendants shall possess it" (ESV).

The Hebrew word for *fully* in this verse reveals in context that it can be understood as "wholehearted."[3] The most important qualifying factor to realizing the God-dream for your life is following fully, without divisions in your heart. Because we are capable of so much, we end up accomplishing so little. Our divided hearts choose everything; therefore, we master nothing. One of the greatest impartations of this book is the concept that you do not have to live in the chaos of infinite choice. You can rest in the singular devotion to God's will that produces one path. To live fully is to live fully devoted to God.

God Uses Inability

When I was eleven years old, I had a bad cold. I was shivering and completely miserable, and my mom laid her hand on me. It was almost like she was receiving information from another source.

She jumped back and said, "Oh, wow—how can it be so?" I remember her saying those words exactly, and then she looked at me and began to cry. She said, "I went to lay my hand on you to pray for your sickness. And I got a vision of you as a grown man, and you are a lead pastor of a church."

That may not seem that miraculous, but let me tell you a bit about who I was as a child. I was so incredibly introverted. I was so scared of people when I was in elementary school, I remember my hand would shake when I would try to drink milk from those little half-pint cartons in the cafeteria.

Anytime anything of spiritual significance happened around me, I literally would run away from it. I didn't want anything to do with it.

So for my mom to have that vision was astonishing; it was so contrary to who I was at the time. But you see, God reserves a destiny for our lives that is contrary to what we think we can do. This keeps us in a posture of surrender, and I think Caleb understood this. He knew there was no way that Israel could defeat Canaan on their own. But he also knew that they could do it with God. He knew if they stepped on the battlefield, then God would show up.

It was the same thing for King David in the Bible. We give him so much credit for having the sling and doing what he did to kill Goliath, but slings don't kill giants. Jesus kills giants!

God makes the impossible possible, and at eleven years old, God wove His narrative into my life. God didn't need my ability. He utilized my *inability* to reveal His glory.

What happens is we get stuck on the road of our own strength rather than the runway of God's empowering ability. We get convinced that it's our ability that's going to accomplish things, but it's through our inability that God accomplishes what He's called us to do. That's why Paul complained about continuing to do things that he didn't want to do (Romans 7:15). He was weak. He was imperfect. But he was surrendered and willing and so in spite of his own shortcomings, God used him.

When we feel that God has given us too much, when we feel that we don't measure up, God increases our capacity. Caleb was at maximum capacity. He went from the road to the runway, and he was rewarded. Joshua 14:13–15 reads, "Then Joshua blessed him, and he gave Hebron to Caleb the son of Jephunneh for an inheritance. Therefore Hebron became the inheritance of Caleb the son of Jephunneh the Kenizzite to this day, because he wholly followed the LORD, the God of Israel. Now the name of Hebron formerly was Kiriath-arba. (Arba was the greatest man among the Anakim.) And the land had rest from war."

The outsider Caleb, the one who took God at his word was willing to live life with God. Caleb got his start much later in life, but he realized that forty-five years spent waiting on the runway is better than forty-five years of striving on the road. He knew that when we are patient, God would have to be a liar to not do what He has promised He will do.

Stay on the Runway

Maybe you've been on the road instead of the runway. Maybe you've never fully chosen to step into God's best for you. You've never chosen the runway.

Or maybe you've been on the runway, and you've been waiting a long time. Maybe it seems that your flight has been delayed over and over again and you're tempted to go back to the road.

Friend, if you really want to go V1, then it's important to get on the runway and stay put.

Caleb was nothing more than a wholehearted guy who believed God at His word and who was willing to wait. He is a great example of what happens when we choose not to be bitter. When we choose to allow the Lord to do His work, in His time. When we trust that God has something great planned, even when we can't see it ourselves.

Everything is on the line, my friend.

If you're in captivity right now, it's because you've been living the lie that the results are one hundred percent based on you. That's called secular humanism. That's called Disney animated films where the characters put in a bunch of work and have their happily-ever-afters.

But the gospel tells us that there is One greater. One who has a plan and a purpose for your life. And when you step out onto His runway, the results aren't your burden to bear. Your only responsibility is to stay on the runway.

God only wants your willingness, and He is speaking to you right now. The ones who are willing to wholly follow the Lord and fight by His side, are the ones who will rest in His blessing.

So when it comes to your marriage, stay on the runway.

When it comes to your calling, stay on the runway.

When it comes to your ministry, stay on the runway.

When it comes to the business God has called you to, stay on the runway.

When it comes to your children, stay on the runway.

When it comes to your home, stay on the runway.

Maybe there's been a multi-generational war going on in your family line, and you inherited alcoholism, you inherited domestic abuse, you inherited negativity and pessimism. But you know you've been called for greatness. You know the promised land is for you, and that all you need to do is stay on the runway and wait for takeoff.

Nobody else might be able to see the evidence of what can come of your life, but God sees it and He's calling you to it! Will you say yes to Jesus and believe like Abraham and Caleb?

Tell God that you're tired of struggling on the road; you're ready for the runway. Tell Him that you're ready to say yes over and over again to what God has for you. Whether takeoff happens tomorrow or ten years from now, you're on the runway and you're staying put.

All you need is a heart that fully and wholly says yes to Jesus.

WORKBOOK

Chapter Five Questions

Question: In your Christian walk, are you striving in your own strength to do the things God has called you to do? How do you know if you are on the road or the runway in your faith walk?

_____

_____

_____

_____

_____

_____

_____

_____

_____

_____

Question: Do you struggle to wait on God and His timing? In what ways has impatience caused you to function in your own strength rather than rely on God's ability?

_____

_____

_____

_____

_____

_____

_____

_____

_____

_____

Action: *Say yes to the runway.* In a notebook or journal, list your insecurities and inabilities. Ask God to show you what He says about you. Write whatever He speaks to you. Invite the Holy Spirit to fill you with His capability and increase your capacity to do and be all God has called you to. Tell God you're ready to say *yes*.

Chapter Five Notes

CHAPTER SIX

The Ten Enemies

I found a video from a preacher online. The video had half a million views—can you believe it?! My initial reaction was to praise the Lord that a preacher's video could reach so many people with the message of God!

Then I clicked on the comments. Every relevant comment bashed this guy brutally. Like we are talking unrelenting mockery and ridicule.

I had to take a step back. It got me wondering—could V1 church withstand the hatred we would receive if we went viral? When I think about Caleb standing before the multitude of people, quieting them down enough to have a captive audience for his audacious speech, I think about how the impossible is possible with God, I realize that not everyone is going to share your enthusiasm.

Psalm 23:5 says, "You prepare a table before me in the presence of my enemies; you anoint my head with oil; my cup overflows." This verse says what we already know. The table of haters is full. But here's the part that we don't always remember: God prepares our provision *in front* of those very people who hate and shame us and attack our enthusiastic declarations of what is possible through God.

You might be on the runway, but you feel stuck. You feel like your relationship with the Lord is in neutral because you just can't shake all of the things that threaten to pull you away from Him. You struggle to follow God every day. You struggle with the voices of the naysayers—the ones who would rather listen to the ten faithless spies than the two faithful ones. Maybe the loud majority has quieted your boldness.

Psalm 23:5 makes it clear that God will give you everything you need to make it through. And more than that, you will be able to prosper in front of the very people and the very things that are currently trying to come against you. The bad report of the ten spies initially spread throughout the people of Israel, but in the end, Joshua and Celeb were vindicated.

Psalm 23:5 is a verse of victory! It's a promise from God! But it's also a verse of discomfort, and that's what we need to talk about.

You see, you have to face your enemies in order to receive provision at God's table. God will serve up everything you need to be strong and chase after your dreams and callings, but He'll only serve you in front of the very people and temptations and processes that cause you concern today.

Some biblical scholars believe that David, the future king of Israel, wrote this psalm before he was ever anointed by the prophet Samuel to become king, while others point to evidence that it was written in the later stages of his life as king.[4]

In other words, David could have written these words before his life changed radically. It could have been a prophetic declaration from a shepherd boy's experiences, who was sitting on the side of a hill, living a very mundane life.

Early on, nobody knew David. Nobody knew his God-given destiny. Nobody knew the greatness within. So at the time when he was a *nobody*—at the time when he didn't have many real adversaries—David knew "the LORD prepares a table before my enemies." The list of enemies changed over the years. He graduated from the lion and the bear threatening his flock, Saul threatening his life, and then eventually, his own son Absalom threatening his title. In every stage of David's life, we see a confidence in God, even while people were failing him.

David knew about the Lord's provision before he even knew how much he would need it. And this very provision is available to you, too. The *sixth step* to go V1 is to sit at a table with ten enemies and claim God's provision and victory over them.

Enemies of Process

There are ten primary enemies of God's process. These enemies are what will make following Jesus so very difficult as you sit on that runway; they will do everything in their power to keep you from going V1. To gain victory of them, God wants you to face them. To sit down and truly face them while you accept the provision He offers.

Think of it like a dinner party, a gathering of your biggest and loudest haters. When you take a seat at that table, here's who you will see.

You will see an enemy named self-pity.

You'll see an enemy named fear.

You'll see an enemy named counterfeit vision.

You'll see an enemy named compromise.

You'll see an enemy named shame.

You'll see an enemy named success.

You'll see an enemy named comfort.

You'll see an enemy named impatience, whose nickname is "no."

You'll see an enemy named inconsistency.

And then you'll see an enemy named selfishness.

And here's the thing. While you're sitting at the table with these ten enemies, staring them down—being strong in their presence and bold in the face of their lies—God will serve up all you need for victory.

So let's unpack that.

Self-Pity

Self-pity is as destructive as narcotics. It's addictive. It gives momentary pleasure while it separates the victim from reality. Many of us take the pill of self-pity, because it feels so good! It allows us to justify our thoughts and actions and prevents any sort of life change.

I was raised in a trailer park on welfare. We paid $15 a month for rent and ended up with some of the most horrific experiences. I clawed my way out of that hole and got a degree from a Big Ten university. I thought for sure that every employer within a ten-mile radius of my house was going to offer me a job before graduation. I thought this, because when you're poor and on the outside looking in on middle class white people, that's what you think happens. That's how you think the world works. Get a degree like the middle-class white folks, and you'll have people begging you to come work for them. Then you can get married, have kids, buy a house, and live happily ever after! Nobody told me that it takes way more than a degree to get hired.

I was stuck sitting at the table with this enemy called self-pity, and I didn't want to eat the confidence God was serving up. So I had to learn the hard way. I had to realize the world does"t owe me anything. It doesn't matter how many degrees you have; you've got to earn everything that comes your way.

But here's the true danger of self-pity: self-pity is excessive, self-absorbed unhappiness that is focused completely on one's own troubles. Romans 8:6 reads, "For to set the mind on the flesh is death, but to set the mind on the Spirit is life and peace."

In other words, focusing on your own carnal desires—what you want, what you need, how you feel—is hostility toward God.

The answer, then, is to submit to the Spirit. The Spirit brings life and peace. It will remind you of the goodness of God even in the face of incredible life troubles. *That* is what God will serve up to you when you face your enemy self-pity.

Fear

Helen Keller said, "Avoiding danger is no safer in the long run than outright exposure. The fearful are caught as often as the bold."[5]

The fearful are caught.

You may think that it's best to play it safe. To avoid risk. To never put yourself too far out there. To always look before you leap. But the person who plays it safe has the same likelihood of getting hit by struggle as the person who runs out ahead of the lightning bolt.

There is a saying, of uncertain origin, that one of the greatest discoveries a person can make is to discover they can do what they were afraid they couldn't do. We all love those videos that show someone excelling beyond what they thought they were capable of. Videos of people beating the odds, overcoming obstacles and changing their lives. But to do this, you have to stare fear down and tell it to step aside. You have to fight it with a heaping serving of faith.

Psalm 27:1 reads, "The LORD is my light and my salvation; whom shall I fear? The LORD is the stronghold of my life; of whom shall I be afraid?"

When the Lord is a constant presence in your life, you will find that you have no one and no thing to fear. You will find that your faith overcomes all of that doubt and uncertainty.

Counterfeit Vision

Counterfeit vision is when you settle for *good* when God calls you to *great.* We like to pretend like everything is good. That everything is fine when it's not. But this mindset is an enemy of God's process.

It's far better to take the ugly and messy over the fake. It's better to go through the stench and the filth and the sweat and the blood and the mess of life and come out with something real than to live a perfectly polished pretend life.

This is why I love New Yorkers. They're so real. They'll cut you off and tell you how they feel, and you aren't left wondering where they stand.

But here's what happens. We say that we want things to be real and authentic, but when it comes to the vision we have for our lives, we settle for what's counterfeit.

Let me tell you a little bit about David, though. According to custom, it was the youngest son's responsibility to watch after the family sheep.[6] So, because he was born the youngest, David was stuck with this task.

His brothers were in the militia, going up against the Philistines (1 Samuel 17). David took a break from watching the sheep to bring his brothers some lunch. He got there, and everyone was fixated on watching the Philistine giant, Goliath, as he taunted Israel over and over again.

They listened to his taunts, but greatness didn't come out of them. See, the taunts of your enemy will reveal whether true greatness is inside of you. How you respond to that situation will show what's on the inside.

So David showed up with lunch and heard Goliath running his mouth. And that's when David stepped away from the earthly destiny that his biological father had given him so that he could pursue his spiritual destiny that his heavenly Father had given him.

Think about it! Every moment that David spent planning for and killing Goliath was a moment *not* spent tending to the family sheep. David could have hidden behind the vision that had been handed to him when he was born the youngest son. He could have said, "Good luck brothers, but I've gotta go tend some sheep!" and no one would have thought any less of him.

But instead, David set his earthly vision and dared to step into his true vision, as leader, as man of God, and as future King.

Whose vision for your life are you living? Is it a counterfeit vision that was handed to you by someone else? Did you go to college because someone in your family told you to? Have you suppressed your desire for mission work because someone thought you should work a nine to five instead?

Are you operating under someone else's expectations and pressure or are you operating under God's power?

Don't get me wrong here. David was faithful to those sheep. But when it came time to set the staff down and be a giant killer, David showed up. The whole story of David and Goliath is a story of stepping away from the natural for the supernatural.

There are some people in my life who never understood why I launched a church. They never understood why I travel to speak, why I do what I do. It never made sense to them. No matter what metric of success I measured it by, they always wanted me to stay within the smallness of their own imagination. But I thank God for the boldness of the Holy Spirit who rises up inside and says, *"Son, despite all your faults and failures to start, despite your introversion, I'm going to use you if you'll say yes."*

Counterfeit vision will lead you down a path that is apart from God's best. And that's why we need to identify it as an enemy of His process.

Compromise

C. S. Lewis said, "Indeed the safest road to Hell is the gradual one—the gentle slope, soft underfoot, without sudden turnings, without milestones, without signposts."[7]

The demon assigned to rob you of what God has given you is offering you a gradual slope away from God's truth. Matthew 6:24 reads, "No one can serve two masters, for either he will hate the one and love the other, or he will be devoted to the one and despise the other. You cannot serve God and money."

Now, this isn't saying that God won't bless you beyond measure. Rather, it says that He will bless you when you serve *Him* and become a conduit for that blessing. God will give you influence so that you can become an echo of freedom, not an echo of your own opinion. He will give you financial resources and wealth to steward in your life so that you can push those things out to others, not so that you can hoard them up.

But we tend to compromise. We think, *"Oh, it's okay if I hoard this for myself,"* or, *"It won't matter if I slide on a few of my commitments to God."*

That approach doesn't work for God, because compromise leads to confusion. This confusion comes from listening to too many voices.

But God has one singular vision for you, and when you're listening to His voice, there will be no confusion. There will be no compromise. What He tells you might not be what you want to hear. It might not be what you want to do, but it will be a singular message that will produce clarity.

Shame

At this dinner party, shame is the guy who tells you that you're not allowed to access your future because of what you did in your past. That's what shame says on repeat. We'll get into this later in the book, but know this: shame will rob you of all confidence. You might know the right thing to do, the right thing to say, but shame will tell you that you aren't qualified.

First John 1:9 says, "If we confess our sins, he is faithful and just to forgive us our sins and to cleanse us from all unrighteousness." Those bad things from your past don't have to define you, because Christ washes you clean.

Micah 7:19 says, "You will again have compassion on us; you will tread our sins underfoot and hurl all our iniquities into the depths of the sea" (NIV). I love the word *again*. It means this isn't a one-and-done thing. So when shame starts talking, you can hear God saying, *"I forgive you. My mercy is here for you. I'm renewing you again."*

God wants to give you honor. He wants to give you favor. He wants you to live in a no-shame zone, even when you're sitting in front of an enemy that does nothing but promote shame. And He offers all the confidence you need to stare that enemy down and put him in his place.

Success

I have an acronym for *haters:*

Having
Anger
Towards
Everyone
Reaching
Success.

Pretty good, right?

Now the good thing about haters is that they're Equal Opportunity Haters. Haters usually hate everyone. No matter how well you do on a job, no matter how much you work it, no matter how transparent or humble you are, no matter how much you strive for excellence, there are people whose favorite pastime is to tear you down.

They do this because your success is a mirror of their failure. And I know this, because I'm one of those people who used to hate on everyone all the time.

Over a decade ago, I built an entire Twitter platform to bash preachers. No joke. Any time a pastor got a bump or some measure of success, and I felt he didn't represent biblical Christianity, I attacked him on Twitter in an attempt to defend those affected by his leadership.

Finally, the Holy Spirit had to deal with me. He showed me that I was attacking others because I felt like a failure. The wounds of my own fatherlessness deeply desired that men of that caliber would reach out to me. What manifested itself as an attack on them was really a cry for help from me. And here's the thing with God: He doesn't just speak into something; He follows up for true healing.

After He spoke to me, He told me that He wanted me to heart, comment, and share every single one of these posts from pastors that I'd been bashing. He wanted me to celebrate them until I learned how to love and celebrate others the way God does.

God showed me that it was by His grace that these pastors were successful, and that any success that I would see would also be by His grace.

No one's story is a straight line. Every one of us has our own winding road that was born out of our pain and the decisions we've made. It may seem like there is no way that you'll arrive at your destination on time. It may seem like success is only something for other people to experience, not you. But I am here to tell you that time is not the same for God. What could take you a lifetime will take Him an instant. He's the one with the controls, and if you submit to Him, you will accelerate to your destiny.

In your moments of failure, instead of listening to the voice of success that makes you envious and down, listen to the God who holds time in His hand.

Comfort

The comfort zone is a psychological state in which one feels familiar, safe, secure, and at ease. It's a place where we love to set up camp, don't we? Comfort is one of my favorite enemies. So fluffy, so nice.

But you can never change your life until you're willing to leave your comfort zone.

You see, leadership is simply somebody who has abandoned comfort over and over and over again. Leaders aren't necessarily smarter than you, they're just a bit more daring than you. They're willing to step out of comfort while the rest of us stay put.

And if you've ever tried to step out of your comfort zone, you'll notice how difficult it is to keep going. You get that first step out of the way and before you know it, comfort comes to you and tells you to just stay put. To create a new comfort zone.

Following Jesus is painful. It's difficult. It's not always fun, but Proverbs 3:5–6 reads, "Trust in the LORD with all your heart, and do not lean on your own understanding. In all your ways acknowledge him, and he will make straight your paths." And that's why you can face comfort and know that God will provide the courage needed to take that step into the unknown.

Impatience

Wise people are careful with their time, but impatience can cause the wise to do foolish things. Impatience is what causes you to leave your marriage right before God is about to heal it. Impatience is what makes you grumble and complain about your job right when you were about to get a promotion. Impatience is what can ruin the good that is about to come your way. In fact, one of the most successful historic strategies of warfare is to wait. Wait until the enemy grows impatient. Once they are impatient, they will make mistakes.

The devil knows this! He taunts you with impatience so that he can pounce. To have victory over this enemy, all you need is to wait on the Lord. He will work in His time, every time.

Inconsistency

Charles Spurgeon once said that inconsistency among Christians is what prevents wicked men from following God.[8] They see us Christians backsliding on the things that we said we would never do, and it pushes them further away from accepting Jesus.

You see the enemy of inconsistency tells you that it's not that big of a deal to stop following Jesus here and there. It's not that big of a deal to slip up every now and again. And before you know it, your witness is blown.

I don't know about you, but I have a vision for men who are going to rise up—not as perfect men, but as men who are submitted to God and going on a journey of maturity. Their very presence will be a conviction of those around them, and their consistency with what they believe will offer a pure conscience in a society where everyone's conscience is being seared.

I have a vision of women rising up, whose very presence signals that God is with them in a palpable way. These women refuse to give in to carnal desire, and they are empowered by the Holy Spirit.

That's my dream for you, for the church. My dream is that the enemy of inconsistency be put to rest as we feast on God's incredible provision to see us through.

Selfishness

Almost every sinful act ever committed can be traced back to a selfish motive. Think about it.

Selfishness is a trait that we hate in other people, yet we justify it in ourselves. But take this to heart: Love is patient. Love is kind. Love doesn't envy. It doesn't boast. It doesn't have to give you a list of qualifications or a list of accomplishments. Love is not arrogant. Love isn't rude. It doesn't insist on getting its own way all the time. Love is not irritable. It's not resentful. It doesn't rejoice in wrongdoing; it doesn't rejoice when someone else fails. It rejoices with the truth (1 Corinthians 13:4–6). And what's the truth? The truth is the cross demands that we accept the reality that the best is yet to come. And the renewal of all things is going to be what we see if we surrender to the cross.

A Seat at the Table

Julie and I made a very difficult decision several years ago. It was something that we wrestled with for a long time as we sought God's will for our lives. After we made this decision, there were many, many people who didn't understand it. They didn't think it was the right thing.

Now these were people that we had served and given our lives to and poured into, and they were coming at us, questioning everything about the decision we had made.

And it hurt. You see we thought we had built up credibility. We thought that these people trusted us and knew us enough to know that we only wanted to follow Jesus. But we were getting slandered and gossiped about, and it was a very dark time.

One night in the midst of that, we went out to eat with our young daughter Bella. Before we knew it, every single person who had bashed us, walked into that very same restaurant. Not only that, but out of all of the tables in the restaurant, they were seated at the one in front of us. Julie and I were sitting side by side, and they were sitting side by side, and we were all just looking at one another.

And while they were looking at us and we were looking at them, a scripture came to mind.

> *You prepare a table before me in the presence of my enemies; you anoint my head with oil; my cup overflows. Surely goodness and mercy shall follow me all the days of my life, and I shall dwell in the house of the LORD forever.*
> —***Psalm 23:5-6***

God prepares a table for us in the presence of these ten enemies—and He provides all that we need to overcome, friend.

Within the last two years, people from that table have called me up individually and told me that they were sorry. They've told me that they can't believe they had acted in that way. They've asked for forgiveness, and we've made amends with every single one.

It's clear. There are true enemies to God's process, but God wants you to be strong against them. Simply rest in Him, eat from the platter of faith, consistency, and empowerment that He is serving up. And trust Him for the rest.

WORKBOOK

Chapter Six Questions

Question: Have you ever come face to face with the ten enemies of God's process? How do you respond when faced with them?

_____
_____
_____
_____
_____
_____
_____
_____
_____
_____

Question: Which of the ten do you believe you are most susceptible to? Have you experienced God enabling you to overcome any of these enemies?

_____
_____
_____
_____
_____
_____
_____
_____
_____
_____

Action: *Sit at the table with the ten enemies and claim God's provision and victory over them.* In a notebook or journal, write each of the ten enemies on a separate page. For each enemy, write a prayer declaring the victory provided by God over that enemy.

Chapter Six Notes

CHAPTER SEVEN

Crossing the Jordan

Change is a good thing, but we never seem to feel that way when it's actually happening. We prefer business as usual. We prefer to go through the motions, but every once in a while, God disrupts our status quo.

And the thing is, we work so hard not to need God. We pop pills and read books and take classes, and all of those things can be good and right but there comes a point when we have to admit that we're out of options and all that's left is to trust God. There comes a point when we have to realize we can't go back to Egypt and slavery. All we can do is go forward with God.

I used to be the person in the back row, judging what happened in church services. I thought that there was no way that the change God offered could actually work. I thought everyone was faking. And then God brought me to a place where there was no other way but to trust. And by His hand, I found myself surrounded by the Father and I've never been the same.

I promise that you'll get to a point where you can't drink your way to the other side anymore. You'll get to a point where you can't even binge-watch your way through it.

In those places, God is waiting for you, and if you step into what He has for you, then you're a candidate for a miracle.

Before we look at Joshua 4, I want to set the scene a bit. Way before Caleb did his thing, there was a man named Moses (Exodus 3–14). Moses went to Pharaoh and demanded that he let the Israelites go and release them from slavery.

Pharaoh resisted; there was a struggle. But in the end, the Israelites followed Moses out of Egypt with the goal of finding God's promised land for them. The Israelites then spent decades wandering around the wilderness until God raised up Caleb to provide a different kind of report on the land of Canaan (Joshua 5:6).

And the only other spy who supported and agreed with Caleb's account of Canaan was a man named Joshua. Joshua would go on to lead the Israelites *into* the promised land.

Now, Joshua wasn't as nice as Moses was. His leadership was black and white. He wanted the heart of God, no deviation. So he brought the people of God to the River Jordan, a massive, intimidating river. On the other side was Canaan, the land God had promised to them. A place of abundance. A reward. The kind of place where you never have to check your bank account again, because prosperity was flowing.

In that moment, Israel was stuck in between. They weren't in slavery, but they also weren't where they should be. And they were tired.

They'd been told about this promised land for so long, it's as if a lot of them stopped believing that it was even possible. Reaching the Jordan solidified this. They looked at how impossible the water was and figured it was the end of the road. There was no way they were getting across to Canaan on the other side.

Worse than being a slave to someone else's vision is trying to do the thing God called you to do and realizing that it's impossible. And I'll be honest. There are days when you're in the midst of your calling, and it's so taxing and difficult, you think about how things were so much easier when you were drunk all the time.

Or there are times when you're in the marriage God has for you, and you'll think about how much easier it was when you were single and took care of yourself first.

Israel experienced this. They got to the Jordan and thought about how much easier they had it in Egypt. In Egypt they knew what to expect.

> When all the nation had finished passing over the Jordan, the LORD said to Joshua, "Take twelve men from the people, from each tribe a man, and command them, saying, 'Take twelve stones from here out of the midst of the Jordan, from the very place where the priests' feet stood firmly, and bring them over with you and lay them down in the place where you lodge tonight.'" Then Joshua called the twelve men from the people of Israel, whom he had appointed, a man from each tribe. And Joshua said to them, "Pass on before the ark of the LORD your God into the midst of the Jordan, and take up each of you a stone

> upon his shoulder, according to the number of the tribes of the people of Israel, that this may be a sign among you. When your children ask in time to come, 'What do those stones mean to you?' then you shall tell them that the waters of the Jordan were cut off before the ark of the covenant of the LORD. When it passed over the Jordan, the waters of the Jordan were cut off. So these stones shall be to the people of Israel a memorial forever."
> —*Joshua 4:1-7*

I want to talk about the shame of our past, the pain from our present, and the promise of the future—and how all of this affects the here and now.

When you accepted Jesus Christ, you got grafted into the family. The history of the Bible, the history of Israel, is your history, too.

Your spiritual family, the children of Israel, came from Egypt and slavery. Now the biblical definition of slavery is when you serve another man's vision instead of God's vision for your life. Here's what that may look like in today's terms:

- If you if you watch pornography, you are serving someone else's vision.

- If you feel pressure to keep up with the Joneses, you're serving someone else's vision.

- If you're driving a car that equals half or more than your total annual income, you're serving someone else's vision. Meanwhile, you're asking God to be generous to you while you've already been generous to the bank!

- If you are serving the God of capitalism, you cannot serve the God of Israel. The Bible says you can't have two masters (Matthew 6:24). You can't *love* money and also *love* God.

The thing I'm getting at is that every one of us has served other masters in the past, if not at this very moment. These masters are cruel. They make us do things we hate, and they make us become people we don't want to become. And that's exactly what happened to the nation of Israel. They were in physical captivity and also spiritual captivity. Their legacy was gone.

Many of us are orphaned in this world, because we never inherited a legacy. We weren't born into values or wisdom. Nothing was passed down to us, and the Bible says that where there is no vision, the people die (Proverbs 29:18 KJV).

But if we can get out of Egypt, we will find ourselves in front of the River Jordan. And it's at that river's edge that we must decide. Do we return to Egypt, back to someone else's vision for our lives? Or do we do the very impossible, hard thing and trust God to get us across the waters? The *seventh step* in going V1 is identifying your River Jordan and inviting Jesus to help you cross those waters.

My River Jordan

After a year and a half of marriage counseling, my wife and I sat in a session in which the counselor told us that we didn't need any more sessions. Can you imagine how freeing that was? It felt like we got off parole! I didn't think it was possible! But then the panic set in.

We couldn't help but ask, "What next? How do we stay married if we're not going to counseling?"

Of course, the counselor reminded me that we had spent the last year and a half figuring that out. We had been given all the tools we needed. The know-how was there. We just needed to keep living it.

Today, people look at Julie and me as marriage role models. We can't believe it! We think of what we came out of, and it's humbling to see how much has changed.

I'll never forget when our marriage finally started to look normal. When we didn't fight at dinner anymore. When peace and calm started to return. And you know what? God showed up. I was getting opportunities to speak, and I was gaining in influence.

On the other side of this I was radically accountable. I ported my phone number over to my wife's phone, so that she was aware of every text and call I received. And over time, God came through. I used to be an example of a broken man, but then God set me free, set my marriage free, and He took us across the Jordan.

The Bible says the Holy Spirit will teach you all things, and I've seen it happen. You see, I had gotten to a point in my marriage where I didn't think I could ever love her again. I knew I could be with her, but I couldn't love her. Not in the way that a husband loves a wife. That just shows you how far we have come.

When people fail at loving you, it's easy to become trapped by the need to please yourself. You think you're helping. You think that some self-care is what you need, when really, you need the Spirit.

Julie failed at loving me. And I certainly failed at loving her. And we had started to focus only on pleasing ourselves. When this happens, you end up building a wall around yourself, brick by brick, so that no one else is able to love you as good as you love yourself. This creates a never-ending cycle, because no one will be able to break through that wall.

I fell in love with my wife again because of the Spirit leading me. I let go of my self-ambition because of the Spirit. You see, I had always been trying to build my own thing, do my own ministry work. I felt like Johnny Cash. A lone ranger. But I was addicted to me, and the Spirit showed me that!

Because of the Spirit, I'm free. My marriage has been saved. My ministry is doing incredible things. I don't hate myself anymore. I don't hurt like I used to. This was my Jordan River.

What's yours? You might be standing on its banks, right now. You know you need to cross it to go V1, but it just looks too impossible.

You might be thinking:

"I don't have the ability, the talent, the money, the resources, the relationships."

"Not a single person in my life has ever crossed this river. Not my grandfather, not my great-grandfather, not a single person."

And I'm telling you it's okay to feel those things. It's expected, even. The only thing that matters is when you can also say, "*I'm not who I used to be. I'm not who I should be. But I believe the promise. I believe I'm getting to the other side.*"

The Power of Presence

When Joshua and Israel came to the River Jordan, they didn't build boats or try doing a human chain or anything like that. Instead, the word of the Lord came down and Joshua was given a revelation to take the Ark of the Covenant, which was housing the glory of God, and put it upon the shoulders of priests and walk it into the waters.

Joshua knew that if they did this, the waters would recede, and the impossible would become possible. So they took the *presence of God* into the waters of impossibility. And the waters receded.

Friend, you've tried it every other way. But I dare you to take God's presence into your situation. I dare you to bring His presence into your life. I dare you to invite his presence into your marriage, into your addiction, right before you get ready to do that habit that you hate.

God's presence used to be confined to the Ark of the Covenant, but today His presence is in us through His Spirit because of what Jesus did for us. When Jesus was on the earth, He was baptized in the River Jordan. The people saw that and remembered what had happened there so many years before. They saw how far they had come, and now it's Jesus who takes us across our own

River Jordans and into the true promised land. He sets us free forever.

There are ministers who do ministry without Jesus. There are worship leaders who lead worship without Jesus. There are husbands and wives doing marriage without Jesus. There are people who climb the ladder without Jesus.

But when people get Jesus, it changes their lives.

You might be on the runway, but if you aren't on the runway with Jesus, then you may as well be back on the road that leads nowhere.

It's time to bring Jesus into your life so that you can give up that desire to return to Egypt when things get rough. He will help you cross the River Jordan; He will bring the deliverance you need so that you reach V1.

Forever Changed

I'll never forget when Julie asked me to hit a bike trail with her. She said she needed to tell me something.

Life had been good; it had been normal. But the moment she said she had something to reveal, my stomach dropped. Maybe things weren't going as well as I had thought.

So we hit the trail, and after a while we pulled off to the side. We sat down together, and she had a journal with her. She held it and said, "Mike, every single time that you verbally abused me, every single time that you made a mistake, every single time that you messed up, I recorded it in this journal."

Now, that thing was *thick*. Packed with all of her grievances against me. Every single thing I had done to fail her.

Shame hit me like a bulldozer. I was looking at the physical representation of my Egypt. The time when I was serving the vision of pornography, the vision of lust and perversion, the vision the world wanted for me. My Pharaoh got me to buy into a value system that wasn't God's value system. And I made a whole bunch of stupid mistakes under Pharaoh's rule.

The things in that journal were recorded verbatim. She said she needed it to prove that she wasn't crazy. To prove that there were major problems. Because you know how it goes: you're with someone who is abusive and condescending, and they tear you down, and before you know it, you're almost brainwashed. You don't know right from left because you don't know what to believe anymore.

She held the journal up. "Even though we finished marriage counseling, I still held onto this journal. There was something inside of me that told me you were going to go back to your old ways. But the Lord told me, Michael, it's time to trust you again."

That moment felt like crossing the Jordan. It was like we were moving from the shame of the past, through the pain of the present, and into the promised land.

You see, I had felt that something wasn't right. Even though the counselor released us. Even though we seemed to be doing okay. I felt a block between me and Julie.

I knew she hadn't forgiven me fully. I knew she hadn't released what had happened. And I knew I didn't deserve her forgiveness. I deserved divorce. And so that's why I waited and prayed and stayed faithful.

And God showed up. God worked the miracle.

That journal represents my freedom. At one point, it represented my past, and now it represents a miracle.

At first, the Jordan was a river of impossibility for Joshua and Israel. But after they crossed over to the other side, Joshua had them put a stone there to remember what happened. The stone would be a reminder to future generations of what happened at the Jordan. The story of God's power and faithfulness would be told.

How might God's power and faithfulness become a legacy in your life? How might it become something that you tell your children and your children's children?

It's time to identify your River Jordan–that final boss in the game of life—and bring Jesus on board so that you can cross the river to renewal.

WORKBOOK

Chapter Seven Questions

Question: *The biblical definition of slavery is when you serve another man's vision instead of God's vision for your life.* Examine the list of what it can look like when you are a slave to something other than God. Are there any ways you can identify that you are enslaved to another master in your life?

_____

_____

_____

_____

_____

_____

_____

_____

_____

_____

Question: What do you believe is your River Jordan—the thing in your life that seems insurmountable? The struggle, habit, sin, or mistake you feel you can never overcome or get through or grow beyond?

_____

_____

_____

_____

_____

_____

_____

_____

_____

_____

_____

Action: Based on your answer to the previous question, invite Jesus to help you cross the waters of whatever your River Jordan is.

Chapter Seven Notes

CHAPTER EIGHT

Shut Up, Shame!

I believe we have a generational gap in this nation. An entire generation of fatherless men are saying, "I want to be a good dad, but I don't know what that looks like."

Children from divorced families have grown up and are saying, "I want to be in a forever marriage, but I don't know what that looks like." People from broken homes are saying, "I want to be loving and caring to my spouse, but I don't know what that looks like." New church members are saying, "I want to be in a healthy church body, but all the churches I knew when I was a kid were in it for the wrong reasons."

This is where shame sets in. Shame convinces us that our past overshadows our present. It tells us that we'll never measure up and that God's promises don't apply to us because of what we've done or what we've been victims of.

It's the opposite of wanting to return to Egypt; it's when the shame of Egypt prevents us from entering our future.

But Jesus wants to break through that. He says if you do your part, He'll do His. If you stand at the River Jordan, He'll part the waters. If you're willing to be a vessel, God will show up.

Israel struggled with this. They were God's chosen people and yet the shame that they carried from their past prevented them from moving forward. They spent forty years wandering in a wilderness because of it. They got off track over and over again—they didn't know what it looked like to be a people of God, and so they fell away time and again. Finally, God stepped in.

And I am telling you that if He helped Israel when they were stuck, He can help you.

Wandering the Wilderness

> *As soon as all the kings of the Amorites who were beyond the Jordan to the west, and all the kings of the Canaanites who were by the sea, heard that the* Lord *had dried up the waters of the Jordan for the people of Israel until they had crossed over, their hearts melted and there was no longer any spirit in them because of the people of Israel.*
> *—Joshua 5:1*

There is so much truth and revelation to this passage, but you have to know how to unpack it. So let me set the scene for you.

I'm sure we can agree on what a king is. A king is a ruler in a high place. A king is somebody with a lot of influence, a lot of power.

The Amorites were a people who were enemies of Israel (the chosen people of God). Israel had come out of slavery and spent many, many years wandering the wilderness as they struggled to follow God. At this point, their enemies were chasing them, and God miraculously saved the entire nation by parting a sea and allowing them to pass over it, walking on dry land.

Clearly, word spread that the God of Israel had done an undeniable, incredible miracle. When the Amorites heard this, the passage tells us that their hearts melted. I interpret that to mean that they lost their drive; they lost their spirit. They found their morale at an all-time low, and they lost their motivation to continue to harass Israel.

Think about that. The enemies of Israel were broken by what God had done. One miracle set all this in motion. Just one miracle from God.

It's easy to read a passage like this and to think that while it's a nice story, something like that could never happen here and now. But I'm here to change that thinking, my friend.

I want for God to be so powerful in your life that the demonic armies that have been assigned to haunt you find their morale at an all-time low.

I want to inflict depression on the spirit of depression.

I want to give anxiety to anxiety.

I want to start serving up the devil's own meat and food to him so that the demons walking around your city don't even feel like going to work because they'd rather put in their two-week notice and be done with it.

I've had this prayer for my church in Queens, New York. I envision God showing up and putting the devil out of business. I envision this every single Sunday, every single time God moves mightily, and even when we don't see Him moving mightily.

And I envision it for your life, too—but here's the reality check. The rest of the passage unpacks what exactly it takes for God to move mightily and get you to *step eight* in going V1, to allow Him to circumcise your heart and heal the shame of your past so that you can enter the promise of your future.

> At that time the LORD said to Joshua, "Make flint knives and circumcise the sons of Israel a second time." So Joshua made flint knives and circumcised the sons of Israel at Gibeath-haaraloth. And this is the reason why Joshua circumcised them: all the males of the people who came out of Egypt, all the men of war, had died in the wilderness on the way after they had come out of Egypt. Though all the people who came out had been circumcised, yet all the people who were born on the way in the wilderness after they had come out of Egypt had not been circumcised. For the people of Israel walked forty years in the wilderness, until all the nation, the men of war who came out of Egypt, perished, because they did not obey the voice of the LORD; the LORD swore to them that he would not let them see the land that the LORD had sworn to their fathers to give to us, a land flowing with milk and honey. So it was their children, whom he raised up in their place, that Joshua circumcised. For they were uncircumcised, because they had not been circumcised on the way. When the circumcising of the whole nation was finished, they remained in their places in the camp until they were healed. And the LORD said to Joshua, "Today I have rolled

away the reproach of Egypt from you." And so the name of that place is called Gilgal to this day.
—*Joshua 5:2-9*

It's easy to read a passage like this and be confused. "It seems like God is punishing them! He had just worked a miracle—why this? Why now?"

The answer to these thoughts is this: you are not going to get to your next assignment until you've been obedient to your last one.

You might be looking for what's next, praying for God to reveal Himself. Meanwhile, God is waiting on you to finish up the task He assigned to you months ago. He still has richness and fullness for you in the here and now.

That's exactly what happened here.

Remember, the people of Israel had come out of slavery in Egypt. They spent years wandering the wilderness as God repeatedly tried to help them reach the land He had promised to them. But the people kept messing up. They kept doing their own thing, and before they knew it, forty years had passed, and they still hadn't reached what God had for them.

People had lived and died and fought entire wars while wandering the wilderness. More than once, the Israelites threatened to return to Egypt, casting aside everything that God had done for the comfort of what they had known for so long. More than once they considered giving up, and so God needed to do something to bring everyone back into the circle for what would be the final leg of the journey.

He needed to do something that would signify discarding the shame of their past and accepting the promise of their identity in God.

While the people who had come out of Egypt had been circumcised, everyone who had been born into freedom hadn't. So, as He often does in scripture, the Lord used circumcision to give that fresh start—that release from past shame—that the people so desperately needed.

Dealing with Shame

God always tries to move us out of shame, through the pain, and into the promise. That's how He works. It's my destiny and it's yours as well. Whatever your shame is, wherever you came from, whatever you've done, *no matter how many times you revert back to old ways,* He wants to move you out of that heavy, dark place.

Your past might look a lot like my past. I grew up in poverty. My home life was extremely difficult, and I spent most of my twenties chasing after the wrong things. Or your past might look worse than mine. The key is that it doesn't matter what your source of shame is—God is calling you out of it.

And once you realize that, be prepared to face the pain of the present. It's an experience that will leave you relying entirely on God to help you through.

This is a tough reality for people like me who like to take care of themselves. I find myself circling the wilderness more times than I care to admit.

But not Joshua. See, before Joshua came around, Moses had been the one leading the people of Israel. He was a different type of leader. A good leader, but different. He tended to give the people what they wanted instead of what they needed, and so that's partly why wandering the wilderness went on for as long as it did.

But Joshua? Joshua was concerned about one thing only: he wanted the approval of God more than the approval of man.

And it was Joshua who helped the people reclaim what God had for them. They had lost their identity in the wilderness, and God used Joshua to help them find it.

You see, somewhere along the way of running from their enemies and camping out in a desert, the people of Israel had stopped the practice of circumcising their males.

This may not seem like a big deal to us, but you have to understand the intention behind circumcision. To circumcise a male was to make a permanent decision that would have eternal consequences. Once that skin was removed, there was no way to reattach it, and so God used that as a covenant between Him and His people.

This meant that when that blood was shed and that action was completed, that person was permanently connected to God through a covenantal relationship. Circumcision had been a way for God to forever bind himself to Israel. It was truly a demonstration of going V1.

In our culture today, it's very rare to come across anything that is forever binding. People get married only to get a divorce. People sign contracts only to fight them in court. But back in Bible times, a covenant relationship was forever, and so that's what Joshua was dealing with. They had forgotten their covenant relationship with God—and here's the twist: while this was happening, God was also calling Joshua to lead Israel into battle.

There's a story in the Bible in which the people of Israel marched around a city called Jericho and the walls came down. It was a complete miracle, and it allowed them to overtake that city.

But what many people skip over is the fact that this very circumcision story was the precursor to that incredible victory at Jericho. Israel was on the cusp of finally taking some ground and claiming the land God had promised to them when all of a sudden, God dropped the circumcision bomb. Right when they were prepping for battle, God asked them to rededicate themselves and reinstate the covenant. God asked them to go V1.

He wasn't going to take them to the next level until they had dealt with their past, with their shame. He wasn't going to move them forward until they had fully entered into their identity as God's chosen people. If they didn't do this, then God's hand would not fully be with them.

They needed to "get right with God" before God would take them to the next level. And the Bible is clear. As soon as they did what God asked, God held up His end of the bargain. Here again is verse nine: "And the LORD said to Joshua, 'Today I have rolled away the reproach of Egypt from you.' And so the name of that place is called Gilgal to this day."

A Fresh Start

God can take you out of Egypt, but He also has to take the Egypt out of you—and that process might look a little like Gilgal. You may have already crossed the Jordan. You may be ready to walk circles around Jericho, ready for the next big miracle in your life. But yet the stench and residue of your past is still on you.

Shame told me that I couldn't possibly be a good preacher, because as I mentioned before, my dad was a murderer. What is shame telling you?

Is it telling you that you can't possibly be a good mother, because you aren't patient enough, you aren't kind enough, you aren't put-together enough, your house is a mess, your kids disobey you?

Is it telling you that your ministry idea will fail because it's too expensive, you don't have the right network, you've never started a nonprofit before?

In all of these areas of life, and in so many others, the voice of shame is in our ear telling us what we can't do. It tells us who we are.

And in this passage, Joshua knew that before his people could enter into what God had for them, they needed to deal with the shame they were carrying around from Egypt in order to go V1. He knew they needed to make a covenant with God, a permanent decision that would serve as a repeated reminder of who they served and what they were about.

> *Put to death therefore what is earthly in you: sexual immorality, impurity, passion, evil desire, and covetousness, which is idolatry. On account of these the wrath of God is coming. In these you too once walked, when you were living in them. But now you must put them all away: anger, wrath, malice, slander, and obscene talk from your mouth. Do not lie to one another, seeing that you have put off the old self with its practices and have put on the new self, which is being renewed in knowledge after the image of its creator.*
> **—Colossians 3:5–10**

In other words, you may have started in Egypt. It's where your parents grew up. It's where your roots are, but it's time to cast it aside and rid yourself of the unhealthy ways of the past. You cannot have the victory of Jericho until you have the circumcision of Gilgal. It's Gilgal where you take the flint knife and you cut away the old life and you stay in that place until you're healed, until the shame is gone.

And then you walk into Jericho, knowing that God is going to give you the victory that you could never give yourself.

From Gilgal to Jericho

What in your life needs to be cut away? What represents the old you, the Egypt in your life?

What is that thing? It's time to name it, because God is not going to let you leave Gilgal and move onto Jericho until you have dealt with that thing. Until you've cut it away. It might be a mindset. It might be a sin. Or it might be a habit. Whatever it is, it is caused by shame in your life.

I used to counsel people with addiction. I had to learn the science behind addictive chemicals and what they do to the body and brain. I learned what happens when you take a drag on a cigarette, how it causes your heart rate to increase. Many pastors preach against smoking, but smoking is just a habit that points to a bigger problem. That "bigger problem" comes when you're so stressed and full of anxiety that all you can think of is, *"If I can only get a cigarette, I'll be okay."*

Soon the cigarette becomes your counterfeit Holy Spirit. It calms you when you need to be calmed. It comforts you when you need to be comforted. You depend on that cigarette, because you don't know how to handle life, you don't know how to handle stress.

Same thing with drinking. If you're a high achieving person, drinking becomes your instant vacation. You don't need to learn how to rest. You don't need to learn how to give it to God. You don't need to learn how to truly unwind. You just drink, and you're teleported there instantly.

What I learned about addictions counseling is that you're never just supposed to remove whatever it is that you're addicted to. You're always supposed to replace, and that's what God did for Israel. He used circumcision to remove their shame, and he replaced it with the promise of Jericho.

So hear me out. God's not trying to take away your cigarettes. God's not trying to take away your alcohol or your workaholism or your adulterous relationship.

He's trying to circumcise your heart so He can replace it with a victory that nobody from your family who came from the previous generation has ever seen before.

He has a Jericho waiting for you. He has it all set up so that you just need to show up and walk around a few times and pray and the walls will come tumbling down.

But first, you need to address your shame. You need to align with Him. You need to circumcise your heart. Only then will God's power flow and topple giants.

WORKBOOK

Chapter Eight Questions

Question: Are there memories from your past or a lingering sense of shame and guilt from past experiencing hanging over you? How does that shame affect your daily life? How does it affect your relationship with God? How does it affect your ministry?

_____

_____

_____

_____

_____

_____

_____

_____

_____

_____

Question: What is the common theme of the things shame speaks over you? What does God's Word say in response to that?

_____
_____
_____
_____
_____
_____
_____
_____
_____
_____

Action: Allow God to circumcise your heart and heal the shame of your past so that you can enter the promise of your future. What in your life needs to be cut away? What represents the old you, the Egypt in your life? It's time to name it and cut it away. It might be a mindset. It might be a sin. Or it might be a habit. Remove it so God can replace it with His victory.

Chapter Eight Notes

CHAPTER NINE

Worship Always Wins

Have you ever argued with someone in your mind? I do this all the time. These fantasy arguments get so heated that I realize I'm actually ticked off at the person when I see them in real life! Sometimes it's as if the person I'm mad at can even sense something's wrong, but no matter how silly it is, all I can think of is the crazy stuff they said in my head.

This is a perfect example of how we can have a physical, actual relationship with someone, and also a relationship in our mind. We have what the relationship actually is, and then also what we think it is.

But I need to point out that no one wins the battles that remain in our heads. No one wins when they're going up against fantasyland and what-could-have-beens, and if-onlys. It's the real-life battles that count.

The Voice of Certainty

> *Now Jericho was shut up inside and outside because of the people of Israel. None went out, and none came in. And the* LORD *said to Joshua, "See, I have given Jericho into your hand, with its king and mighty men of valor."*
>
> **Joshua 6:1–2**

Have you ever felt locked outside of the promise? Have you ever been so close, you can touch it, you can taste it, you can feel it, but you can't obtain it? We talked about that in previous chapters—what it feels like to stand at the banks of the River Jordan.

But here in this chapter, the people of Israel had made it over the Jordan, they had come out of the wilderness, they had been circumcised, and now they were standing outside of the city of Jericho. Waiting.

And that's when God spoke. He went straight to Joshua and basically told him to open his eyes. The battle had already been won.

Imagine God coming straight to you, calling you by name, and telling you that the thing that's in front of you, He's already given to you. That's powerful stuff.

This is how God speaks. Even with the walls of impossibilities still up, He says it's already won.

God is the type to give you a million-dollar dream when you have $0 in your bank account. He is the type to take someone who has been through countless hurtful and abusive relationships and prepare them for a mate.

While the walls of impossibility are erected around the very thing that God is speaking to your life, He will tell you He already gave it to you. Let me put it like this. You will be taking the medication for the incurable disease when God says He's going to heal you because He's already paid the price for that healing. *"Even with the walls up, I've already given it to you. It's paid for."*

You have the receipt, my friend. Jesus paid for your health, your future. The fight is fixed. Victory is on its way. This is what He was telling Joshua! And when you've crossed the River Jordan and are standing in front of Jericho, it's what He's telling you.

The *ninth step* to go V1 is to find your word from God and your song as you topple the walls of your personal Jericho through worship.

Remembering Whose You Are

> *"You shall march around the city, all the men of war going around the city once. Thus shall you do for six days. Seven priests shall bear seven trumpets of rams' horns before the ark. On the seventh day you shall march around the city seven times, and the priests shall blow the trumpets. And when they make a long blast with the ram's horn, when you hear the sound of the trumpet, then all the people shall shout with a great shout, and the wall of the city will fall down flat, and the people shall go up, everyone straight before him."*
>
> —*Joshua 6:3–5*

Your destiny is in what you repeatedly do.

I remember when I was in Queens, I would do prayer walks every single day. I would walk through the neighborhood and pray that God would raise up a life-giving church there. And all of a sudden, the walls came down, the movie theater doors opened, and God said, *"Let there be church."* God is doing something in Queens.

With Joshua, God commanded that they march around the city of Jericho, once a day for six days. He commanded that seven priests carry ram's horn trumpets in front of the Ark. And on the seventh day, God wanted them to blow the trumpets and a long blast from the ram's horn. At that point the people were to shout, and the city wall would collapse.

God doesn't tell us what He's *thinking* of doing. He tells us what He's about to do.

Certainty is the language of God.

> But Joshua commanded the people, "You shall not shout or make your voice heard, neither shall any word go out of your mouth, until the day I tell you to shout. Then you shall shout."
>
> —*Joshua 6:10*

> On the seventh day they rose early, at the dawn of day, and marched around the city in the same manner seven times. It was only on that day that they marched around the city seven times. And at the seventh time, when the priests had blown the trumpets, Joshua said to the people, "Shout, for the LORD has given you the city. And the city and all that is within it shall be devoted to the LORD for destruction."
>
> —*Joshua 6:15–17*

When Joshua repeated the orders of the Lord in that last verse, he also repeated the certainty that came with them. He said, "All that is within it *shall be* devoted to the LORD" (emphasis mine). He was expressing V1-level devotion to the Lord.

Up to this point, Israel had only fought the battle in their minds. They had been in slavery, then in the wilderness where they forgot who they were, they forgot the covenant. They had come so far, and this moment had built up so much. So the command to walk around the city six times wasn't for Jericho. It wasn't for the battle.

The command was for Israel. You see at this point, Israel was still confused about their identity. All they knew was turmoil and hardship and war. They didn't know what to do with victory.

If your marriage has lasted longer than your parents' marriage, then you know how this feels. If the business you started in your garage is doing better than any of the companies that you previously worked for, then you know how this feels. If you've ever gone to a place in life—academically, vocationally, spiritually—where your parents, grandparents, aunts, and uncles have never been before, then you know how this feels.

Victory and breaking the chains of the past is something to celebrate, but it's also confusing. It's scary. It feels like you're moving blind through life, doing the best you can without a guide to help you.

There comes a burden with being "the first" to do something in your circle of friends and family. Israel was in that position, and they'd been expecting a major battle. They'd been preparing for blood and death and an actual fight to overtake Jericho.

And then God had them circumcised and dropped the bomb that they'd defeat Jericho by marching and eventually with praising.

You see, the way that God wants you to fight your battles doesn't look anything like how *you* want to fight them.

Every time they walked silently around the city of Jericho, it was an assessment. God was demanding that they watch, that they pay attention. That they sit in silence and reflect. He wanted them quiet enough that they were acutely aware of how impossible defeating the city really was. How there was no way that they could do it in their own strength.

Here's a common way we fight our battles: if I yell at Julie loud enough and I articulate it well enough, she will change, and our marriage will get better. That's how we fight our battles. That's what works.

Another way we fight is, when we begin to feel stressed, we turn to food or something that makes us feel good. We get a hit of that dopamine and tryptophan, and we feel better. It's funny—we can't make it to the prayer line, but we can make it to the McDonald's line!

Another thing we do is we throw ourselves into retail therapy. I remember when we moved, and I was unloading our closet. I was shocked at the number of clothes that still had tags on them. I showed them to Julie. "We'd had a hard day," was her response. And isn't it just like humanity to assume that we can't afford counseling, yet we can afford a few new shirts.

Here's what I'm getting at. When we try to fight Jericho-sized battles the way that we usually fight battles, it's never going to work. Our bank accounts aren't big enough, our relationships aren't fulfilling enough, our addiction isn't satisfying enough, our education isn't deep enough. There is nothing within our earthly resources that will bring those walls of impossibility down.

So that's why God gives us seasons of silence. It's so that the reality of just how impossible victory is, sets in. God wants to make sure that when we go V1, He's the only one getting the credit.

No Matter the Cost

All of this is really easy to accept until you have to head back home to the spouse who is verbally and emotionally abusing you.

It's easy to accept until you're within reach of your heroin stash.

I used to be addicted to alcohol. God delivered me from it, but when the pressures of life would mount up, you'd better believe I thought about going back.

See, salvation happens in an instant. But freedom is a journey. Sanctification is a journey. When you turn your life around, those temptations don't end. They still call to you, inviting you back to your old habits. But here's how you know that you're being sanctified.

I'd go into the club, and it was like everything stopped. It felt like the lights had been turned on and I could see everything for what it really was.

You see, I had gone to the club with the intention of living in my old ways. But I was being sanctified, and so when I stepped into my old habit, it didn't look the same. Didn't feel the same. It doesn't bring pleasure anymore.

Has this happened to you? Have you ever started to engage in the habit you hate, and you're right in the middle of that ritual of sin, and something inside of you says, *"I can no longer find pleasure here. I can no longer remain in this place"*?

You may not feel like a great Christian, but you know that you're not where you used to be! You see how far you've come. That's exactly where Israel was in Joshua 6.

Jesus Himself said that no one builds a house without first calculating how much it will cost (Luke 14:28). There will always be a cost to following Jesus, but God is looking for people who will say, "I'm in, no matter what."

The people of Israel were finally *in* no matter the cost. They had been circumcised. They had been through the wilderness. And if they needed to walk around a city in silence, they were willing to do that, too.

Silence Breaks Through

Silence is a time of meditation. It's a time of observation, where you take a step back and reflect on life. It's in moments of silence that you realize maybe you shouldn't be with your current friend group. Maybe you shouldn't be with the person you're dating. Those people might fit your past, but they don't fit your future.

It's in moments of silence that you realize that you don't fully know who you are, but you know more than you knew yesterday.

Maybe this is the first time you've ever stayed married, instead of running away. Maybe this is the first time you've ever stayed on the job instead of quitting. Maybe this is the first time you've ever stayed in your rightful position long enough to observe, to assess, to contemplate, to have that moment of silence.

This is the first time you've stayed put on the runway! The plane is moving. It's gaining speed. And you have a choice to make.

You're staring at your Jericho, and it's not the battle of sin. It's the battle of salvation. It's the battle for legacy. It's a battle for ministry. It's the battle for God's kingdom and His reign in your life. It's a battle for that promised land.

If you feel something inside of you kicking and screaming to be let out, those are your gifts, your visions, your dreams. They are the full potential of what God made you to be, and they will be unleashed once Jericho comes toppling down.

You see, God didn't create us to be mediocre, and that's what the people of Israel were realizing. They had come so far and weren't going to quit.

The plane was taking off. And if marching in silence was what it would take, they were willing to do it.

What Jericho Can Teach Us

If this is you. If you've crossed the River Jordan and are now facing a battle for your future, there are three key things that Jericho teaches us.

First, your enemy shouldn't be the focus. Your focus should be on the change the Lord wants to work through you.

At Jericho, Israel marched around the walls in silence, because the focus wasn't on the enemies inside the city. The focus was on God.

What would the American church be if we stopped saying, *"How can God fix the church?"* And we started saying, *"How can God fix me?"*

This spirit of focusing on others instead of our own relationship with God has robbed us of getting to the next level, of defeating Jericho.

What if you stopped blaming your way around the mountain and started *worshiping* around the mountain? All this requires is a shift in the words you say. Instead of wasting your words on your problems, you send them up to your Father. When words go up, blessings come down. You want spiritual rain? Let the words you say go to heaven and bring a blessing down for you.

God changed me when I stopped praying that God would change my wife. Instead, I started to ask Him to change *me*. And when my wife started praying that God would change *her,* that's when He did it. That's when our marriage shifted and began to heal.

Second, when you fight a battle, you need a word and a song. At first Israel thought they needed a sword and a shield. Makes sense, right? But God works in His way! You may think you need a bigger bank account or friends in high places or whatever it may be, and God says *no.* You only need a word and a song.

The *word* was released to Joshua when God gave His promise of deliverance and victory. And then right before the walls came down, they shouted and released a song, and it was with that song that freedom came.

And last, worship always wins. This is how we fight our battles. Through worship.

My wife has been going through a health battle and it's been one of the most perplexing things we've ever faced. She's a long-distance runner, and she ran twenty-seven miles the week before she got sick over a year ago. She went from distance running to being in excruciating pain.

There came a point in her frustration when she didn't think she could do it anymore. She had reached her limit.

And when she was in that moment, a woman from our church who didn't necessarily know where Julie was at, sent her a word and said, *"I see a wall of fire around your health."*

That lifted Julie spirits, and Julie said, *"Okay, I've got my word. Now I just need a song."* And then Julie got that song. Psalm 27:13, "I believe that I shall look upon the goodness of the LORD in the land of the living!"

The intention behind this Psalm is that we shouldn't let the news change our opinion of God. We shouldn't let our family change our opinion. We shouldn't let circumstance or hardship change our opinion. We are to believe God, no matter what.

So Julie received her song, and we raised a hallelujah so often that my five-year-old knew the words to the Psalm. Friend, this is how we fight our battles: with a word and a song!

Of course, with Julie's illness, we went to the specialists in Manhattan. We did all the things they said to do, but nothing worked. Then I suddenly received an invitation to go to St. Louis, because there was a revival happening at Faith Church. I had already felt like God didn't want me to travel for several months, and I was being obedient to that. But what I didn't know was that He was keeping my schedule clear because He had some better plans.

We got to St. Louis, and we met with the pastors, who were seeing almost twenty thousand people in regular weekly attendance. God was at work there! And they were helping us, they were training us, they were mentoring us so that we could bring a bunch of good things back to New York, and then things got real. They sensed a barrier. And they point-blank asked us what it was.

Julie broke down. She told them about her health. Before we knew it, the pastors arranged for us to see a doctor in town—one that they highly recommended.

The Bible says, "For my thoughts are not your thoughts, neither are your ways my ways, declares the LORD" (Isaiah 55:8). God moves in his time and in His way. We had a word and a song, and we walked into that doctor's office. And it's as if the walls came down.

We told him what had been happening, and his jaw practically dropped to the floor. He told us that he specialized in treating all of her symptoms. He was the perfect person to help.

He told us that he would bet his entire practice that he knew what was going on with her. He said that with treatment, she could be healed within thirty days, and he encouraged us to start treatment before the test results even came back—that's how confident he was. Then he sent Julie out to do bloodwork and get x-rays, and he turned to me and said he didn't want to psych Julie out, but he believed that once we started treatment, she would feel better within forty-eight hours.

We started the treatment, and he was right. Within two days, Julie woke up and felt amazing. She's continuing her journey of healing, but hers is a story that proves worship always wins. We were at our wits' end. We didn't know how it was going to work out. We didn't know what was going to happen. All we knew is that when you get a word from God, you stand on that word. Then you get a song and you just keep walking around those walls, telling God that when He wants you to shout, you're going to shout and trust.

A Word and a Song

Maybe you've already received the word, and the only other thing that is missing is the song. If you feel like you've been walking around the walls of impossibility, trying to do it without Jesus, now is time to make a change.

If you've been walking around the walls with an on-again, off-again relationship with Jesus, now is the time to make a change. If you've received the word, but are missing the song, now is the time to make a change.

It's going to feel vulnerable, but the way up in God's kingdom is down. We fight our battles by giving them up to the Lord. It defies logic, but God transcends logic. The way to go V1 is to trust God's Word and sing a song of praise.

WORKBOOK

Chapter Nine Questions

Question: Has God given you a specific word or promise for your life? If not, ask Him to give you one. Write down what He speaks to you.

_____
_____
_____
_____
_____
_____
_____
_____
_____
_____

Question: Examine where you are at in your life today. Can you see evidence of how far God has brought you? Are you further along than you were yesterday, a month ago, a year ago, or five years ago?

_____
_____
_____
_____
_____
_____
_____
_____
_____
_____

Action: Find your word and your song as you topple the walls of your personal Jericho using worship. For whatever setback you are facing right now, ask God to give you a word and a song for it. Then continue to speak that word and sing that song daily.

Chapter Nine Notes

CONCLUSION

Point of No Return

My pilot friend Micah—the pilot I met in a restaurant—said something very profound to me. He said that one mile of road will take you one mile, but one mile of runway will take you anywhere.

Friend, I want to welcome you to the runway.

On the runway, not even a long delay can prevent you from reaching your destination. I've been on flights where the pilots have still landed us on time, even though we were on the runway for hours. They push the plane and make up for lost time, and that's what I want you to take to heart: it's time to make up for lost time.

It's time to break the chains that have kept you from flying. Who you were yesterday—who you were a moment ago—does not need to dictate who you are in this moment. Maybe you've been slipping back into addiction. Maybe you've been retreating into comfort. Maybe you've been saying that you're done with the promised land; you're tired of the struggle to make it there.

God is saying that it doesn't matter what you've done, where you come from, or what your issues are. He wants you to take back the promise. He wants you to consecrate yourself to Him, to believe Him at your River Jordan, and to topple your Jericho with a word and a song.

God is ready to restore you. He's ready to cleanse you.

His forgiveness is not like anything you've ever experienced. And His power is unmatched.

Watch Him overwhelm you with His love, goodness, and acceptance. Watch him lavish love on you. Watch Him break through your layers of pain and layers of rejection. Watch Him prove that He can do for you what He did for Caleb, for Joshua, and for all of Israel.

Watch Him take you V1.

Heavenly Father,

I thank You for everything that's come through my life. I thank You, because I believe You will take what was meant for harm and turn it around for my good. I choose to go V1 today. I choose to believe that You have called me to do great things. I cast off the old. I put on the new. Wash me with Your blood, Jesus. Make me clean in You. Set my feet on solid ground. Take me off the road and place me on the runway. Turn on that engine, and let's go, Lord. I'm all in.

REFERENCES

Notes

1. Plato. *The Apology of Socrates.* Strelbytskyy Multimedia Publishing, 2020.

2. Herder, Johann Gottfried. *The Spirit of Hebrew Poetry.* E. Smith, 1833.

3. Blue Letter Bible, "Strong's H4390 – *mālā*." https://www.blueletterbible.org/lexicon/h4390/kjv/wlc/0-1/.

4. Burnette-Bletsch, Rhonda. "Psalm 23." Bible Odyssey: Ask a Scholar. https://www.bibleodyssey.org/tools/ask-a-scholar/psalm-23.

5. Keller, Hellen. *Let Us Have Faith.* Doubleday & Company, 1946, p. 50–51.

6. Wight, Fred H. *Manners and Customs of Bible Lands.* Moody Press, 1953.

7. Lewis, C. S. *The Screwtape Letters.* 1941. HarperCollins, 2001, p. 61.

8. Spurgeon, Charles Haddon. *Sermons Preached and Revised by C. H. Spurgeon.* Sixth series. Sheldon, 1860, p. 134–135.

About the Author

Mike Signorelli is the founding pastor of V1 Church. In just five years, V1 Church grew from one location to three campuses nationally across New York Metro, Brooklyn, and Indiana; including over 100 watch parties globally in homes. According to INJOY Stewardship Solutions, V1 Church achieved the "Fastest-Growing Church in America" category for three consecutive years. During the pandemic, Mike started a teaching broadcast online that grew from 20 viewers to over 5 million per month across Facebook, Instagram, and Youtube simulcasts. As a result, V1 College was established to provide leadership and theological training. While only in the second year of operation, V1 College has 136 students enrolled from 16 nations. Mike and his wife Julie have a passion for healthy marriages and relationships and share their story of healing—particularly in underserved populations with limited access to professional care. Their most recent marriage conference hosted over 2,500 couples as they renewed their vows.

Seeing many struggle for basic necessities in New York City Metro, Mike and Julie responded with the creation of a non-profit called Operation Impact. Each Christmas, hundreds in shelters between Brooklyn and Long Island are provided with a Christmas miracle! Operation Impact has recently expanded to 5 countries as radical generosity spreads through partnership. In addition, multi-site food distribution, backpack drives, and coat drives provide for many year-round. Mike and Julie have two daughters—Everly Faith and Bella Joy. They currently reside in Queens, NYC where you'll find them discovering new restaurants, ice skating, driving to ballet rehearsal, or laying around at a beach.

About Renown Publishing

Renown Publishing was founded with one mission in mind: to make your great idea famous.

At Renown Publishing, we don't just publish. We work hard to pair strategy with innovative marketing techniques so that your book launch is the start of something bigger.

Learn more at RenownPublishing.com.